THE CHURCH AS MISSION

THE CHURCH
AS MISSION

Eugene Hillman, C.S.Sp.

HERDER AND HERDER

1965
HERDER AND HERDER NEW YORK
232 Madison Avenue, New York 10016

Imprimi potest:	Constantine Chronis, C.S.Sp.
	Superior, Kilimanjaro District
Nihil obstat:	Robert N. Roach, C.S.Sp.
	Censor Deputatus
Imprimatur:	✠ Dennis V. Durning, C.S.Sp.
	Bishop of Arusha
	February 22, 1965

The *Nihil obstat* and *Imprimatur* are official declarations that a book or pamphlet is considered to be free from doctrinal or moral error. No implication is contained therein that those who have granted the *Nihil obstat* and *Imprimatur* agree with the contents, opinions, or statements expressed.

Library of Congress Catalog Card Number: 65–21946
© 1965 by Herder and Herder, Incorporated
Manufactured in the United States of America

CONTENTS

Come over into Macedonia and help us.
Acts 16:10

PREFACE

In the very first line of the Second Vatican Council's *Dogmatic Constitution on the Church* we are reminded that "Christ is the light of nations." The Church is therefore seen as "the universal sacrament of salvation," to become firmly and indigenously established among all peoples. This is why the Church exists, that through her all of God's children should be gathered together sacramentally into one new people. The *Constitution* goes on to tell us that this "messianic people, although it does not actually include all men, and at times may look like a small flock, is nonetheless a lasting and sure *seed* of unity, hope, and salvation for the whole human race." And this community of explicit faith, established by Christ for all men, "is also used by Him as an instrument for the redemption of all, and is sent forth into the whole world as the light of the world and the salt of the earth."

So the whole Church is essentially missionary, and her primary concern is to become actually in the sight of all peoples what she is by her very nature. Indeed, she is the sign of unity to be raised up among the nations, inviting all who have not yet believed, and gathering them into one visible fold. She is the signal of hope, beckoning to the peoples all around, and calling back Israel's new sons from the four corners of the earth. She is the sacrament of salvation, signifying the deliverance of all men, and completing sacramentally what Christ has done "once for all" through His life and death and resurrection. The victory of Christ has already been achieved, but this good news has not yet reached all men.

The new people of God is still scattered among the nations, for the sacramental symbol of their salvation has not yet been raised up for a witness among all peoples. What, then, is the very first duty of those of us who, through explicit faith in Christ, have already seen this light? It is to work for the extension of the Church to the "tribes and tongues and peoples and nations" among whom Christ's saving presence has not yet been signified by the visible Church established among them on firm and indigenous foundations. Such, above all, is the missionary task of the Church. Everything else, in the order of Christian organization and activity, finds its true place only within this missionary orientation of the whole Church which "takes its citizens from every race . . . and is made up from different peoples," to quote again from the *Constitution:*

All men are called to belong to the new people of God. Wherefore this people . . . is to be spread throughout the whole world and must exist in all ages, so that the decree of God's will may be fulfilled. In the beginning God made human nature one and decreed that all His children, scattered as they were, would finally be gathered together as one. It was for this purpose that God sent His Son . . . that He might be the Head of the new and universal people of the sons of God.

All Christians are called to be Christ's witnesses among the nations. Our commitment to this mission is the justification of our own faith, and it is the manifestation of our own hope for salvation. So Pope Pius XII could say of a Christian community that "their growth in holiness will be in proportion to their active interest in the holy missions." And again: "The missionary spirit and the Catholic spirit are one and the same thing." Therefore, to ask the question, "Why the missions?" is at the same time to ask, "Why the Church?" In seeking the answer, we find ourselves also asking the more personal question, "Why

have I been chosen to live visibly among the people of God?";
and we begin to realize that our own salvation hinges on the
answer we give, not in our words only but also by our deeds.

The author of this book has already given his answer by his
deeds as a missionary of the front lines. By his own colleagues
in the field Father Hillman is recognized as a missionary's
missionary. This man of action now offers us his reflections on
the theology of the missions. What he has to say is inspired by
actual experience and charged with a genuine sense of urgency, as
he speaks to us from the heart of Africa where time is running
out in what had promised to be the most abundant harvest in
the missionary history of the Church, but where the laborers
have been too few. This is the same sense of urgency which is
found also in the plea of Pope Paul VI that more priests should
be sent to Africa without delay: "today, not tomorrow . . . for
this may be the moment of grace that could pass forever, never
to return."

Father Hillman shows us how this also may be our "moment
of grace." Will the whole Church respond generously to the
challenge of the missions, not only in Africa but throughout the
world, among the peoples who have not yet seen the light of
nations? Can there be an adequate response without a theological
reëvaluation of our missionary motivation in a world where an
ever increasing majority of men must live and die with no one to
tell them of Christ? Hence the great importance of this book.

✠Richard Cardinal Cushing

Foreword

The thoughts offered for consideration in this book are of great importance. A precise definition must be given to just where the difference lies between the Church's "mission" among "Christian" peoples and that among peoples for whom Christianity does not actually exist. There is such a difference; but its exact formulation is not easy. I agree completely with Father Hillman that the immediate and foremost task of the Church in the mission field is not the saving of individuals, not even of many individuals. And I am glad that a missionary has said it, because I myself, for having said this in treating of "anonymous Christians," have been vigorously attacked by some missionaries.

At the same time, we recognize the fact that it is indeed the task of the Church (because the one is contained in the other) to form as many explicit Christians as possible among the peoples of the world. We cannot some day say: "Right, so we've got a little indigenous Church rooted here among this people, so now the Church in this particular place need not exert itself to convert any more of this people. It is enough if the Church merely continues to exist as a holy remnant among this people, promising the salvation of all." Rather, the Church in each and every region must always want to increase.

It is also difficult to formulate clearly the truth that the regional Church among a particular people is the sign of salvation for all of the people of this nation, including all of its past and present and future members. In *sensu positivo*, this is very true and it is of great importance for mission theology. But in *sensu exclusivo,* it really is not true. That is, one cannot say that Christian salvation is closed to all the members of a people among whom the visible Church is not now, or later, raised up. For then, what of those peoples (quite apart from other reasons) who perished as ethnic-culture units before the advent of Christ? Or what of those who may lack such a presence of the Church even until the return of Christ? Is there any *a priori* conflict here with the theology of salvation? Perhaps there is; but to me it does not seem to be the case.

The Church exists as a continuation of the incarnation of the Logos in the "oneness" of mankind to which all peoples and nations belong; and while this process is going on, the "sacramental" sign of salvation is already present for all people. But this sign for all men must make itself visible in every nation as such, and among all peoples as distinctive units; for it is precisely this physical tangibility of salvation which must be presented among all men as clearly as possible, as historically as possible, indeed in the very "flesh" of each people's history.

Mission theology must emphasize that it is not the first and immediate task of the Church, as the *visible* institution for salvation, to save individuals who can be saved anyway by God through Christ without their being *visibly* in the Church, and who can be thus joined to His Mystical Body. (He does thus save, even though we have no guarantee of salvation respecting any individual.) The prior task of the Church is rather to be the presence of Christ among all nations, the sacrament of salvation for those very people who do not yet belong visibly to the Church. These are the questions that Father Hillman discusses admirably in his book. They are very, very important considerations; as are also his conclusions.

KARL RAHNER, S.J.

13

Author's Introduction

With so many competent Christian scholars writing these days on the nature of the Church, it might be wondered why a missionary in the field should decide that he has something to add which other authors presumably have missed. "Why the missions?", which is the basic inquiry of this book, is moreover a rather bold question to be asking at this late hour in the history of Christianity. Yet the difficulty experienced repeatedly by the Fathers of the Second Vatican Council in their efforts to reach agreement on the several "mission schemas," which were proposed merely as outlines for discussion, suggests that there is room for much more investigation into this question.

In trying to find a satisfactory answer, one learns very quickly that there has been relatively little theological investigation of the specifically missionary character and function of the Church. What little that has been done is for the most part available only in the theological journals of continental Europe, and is, therefore, hardly accessible to the many concerned Christians in the English-speaking world, or to most missionaries in the field. Even the specialized study of missiology is itself a science of recent origin, still seeking its own relevance in the labyrinth of primary research, and greatly in need of contributions from theologians, Scripture scholars, historians, and social scientists.

The reflections of the non-specialist in all of these fields should, therefore, be of some interest, even though his only real claim to a hearing is his own missionary experience and total personal involvement. This book seeks to be just such a contribution.

Far from pretending to be the last word on the subject, the considerations offered here are rather in the nature of tentative and slightly provocative probings, that may lead to an answer in which the teachings of Scripture, tradition, and contemporary theology may be reconciled, if not fully synthesized. And this effort is made with the conviction that the Church's understanding of her universal mission should be intelligible, from existing data and sources, even to Christians who are not themselves professional scholars. It would be a mistake to think, as Karl Rahner has pointed out, that what Scripture and tradition have to say to us can be understood, and must first be interpreted for us, only by specialized students of the various theological disciplines.

The focus of attention in this book is not on the peoples among whom the Church has already become an indigenous and self-sustaining entity, except insofar as these peoples are called to share their faith with those who have not yet known Christ. In emphasizing the urgency of the apostolate to the non-evangelized, and in considering the existing Christian community only in relation to this, there is no intention of minimizing the gravity of the problems that face the Church in Europe and the Americas, or of belittling the work being done by Christians in these areas. It is just that one can neither say everything nor qualify adequately every statement in a single book. Moreover, many excellent works have already been written on the pastoral and social problems of the Church within the cultural sphere of Western Europe, and these problems are actually being attended to on an unprecedented scale—while this is not the case regarding the peoples elsewhere for whom the Church has not yet existed tangibly. Some emphasis on the religious role of these peoples is overdue.

15

So, if the approach of this book may seem excessively influenced or even somewhat prejudiced by more than a dozen
years lived by the author among non-Christian peoples in Africa,
this was not consciously intended. The partial views of men,
but not of gods, follow inevitably from the situation in which
each man finds himself. This may be the very reason why so
many Christian writers in Europe and America have been so
astonishingly inarticulate about the vast majority of mankind
outside their own little flock. And perhaps this also explains the
growing tendency, originating in France, to reduce missionary
activity to the shepherd's task of searching out the "lost sheep"
and the "other sheep" within the milieu, the parish, the diocese,
the nation, while relatively little attention is given to the other
"tribes and tongues and peoples" who have not yet been
evangelized at all. What we must come to understand is that
the Christian community is called into existence from and for
non-Christian peoples, so there is between the two a vital relationship of inter-dependence and of mutual completion.

Acknowledgements and thanks are due to many people, non-
Christian as well as Christian, who contributed in various ways
to the development of the ideas and to the final production of
this book. But special mention should be made of two persons,
each standing appropriately as symbols for all the others. Nagudana, son of Sungwia, is an illiterate and "pagan" warrior
of the Masai tribe of northern Tanzania. Through his friendship, I was led into another world of cultural and spiritual
values, including the primordial monotheism, which I might
otherwise never have known. In the cultural-religious predica-
ment of this person, I had my first real confrontation with the
question which this book attempts to answer. Nagudana stands
for many good people who have been my teachers. And so does

16

Karl Rahner, who patiently answered the inquiring letters I wrote to him from Africa, and who humbly gave me many hours of his time when I visited him in Germany. Without his personal encouragement and guidance, I probably would never have dared to undertake this venture into the theology of missionary activity.

EUGENE HILLMAN, C.S.SP.

Catholic Mission
P.O. Monduli
Tanzania

I.

The New Approach

Little advances and shifts in the field of theory . . . are not often of immediately evident importance. At first, these changes may look more like passing fashions or scholarly quibbling. But if we realize that these new insights enter the common consciousness and become the unquestioned suppositions which are the basis for our action, then we may begin to see that a great deal, sometimes everything, depends on them.

KARL RAHNER

The Church is essentially missionary because the messianic people of God is, and is to become ever more fully, the sacramental light of nations. This dynamic notion of the Church is rooted in Scripture, and it is officially formulated in the Second Vatican Council's *Dogmatic Constitution on the Church*. But this is not a new idea. It is found also in the juridical and organizational structure of the Church's missionary activity directed to the non-evangelized peoples; and it is found in the several encyclical letters and papal directives dealing specifically with this topic. Yet something new is appearing. An increasing number of contemporary writers, both Catholic and Protestant, are presenting a rather different concept of missionary activity; and this has already become, in many areas of Christian action and Church organization, an unquestioned supposition.

Let us make no mistake about it. What is being proposed by these writers is not merely a renewal of our previous understanding of missionary goals, but something quite novel. The implications of this new thought may prove to be very far reaching, if these recent "reëvaluations" are correct. Father George Naidenoff, for example, tells us that "the geographical notion of the missions, founded on the distinction between the evangelizing countries and those being evangelized, is being erased with each passing day, and simply marks a stage in the spiritual impregnation of the universe."

"The geographical notion of the missions," is the new way of referring to our customary understanding of the Church's missionary function. But let it be said at once that this primary and traditional activity has never been directed specifically to geographical localities. For the past four hundred years at least, it has been directed both in theory and in practice to the "tribes and tongues and peoples" who have not yet known Christ through the preaching of the Gospel and the establishment of the Church among them on firm and indigenous foundations. If the achievement now appears to have been less than notable in its effects both among those evangelizing and those being evangelized, we might do well first to seek the reasons for failure in ourselves before deciding simply, in a moment of zeal, to replace the old missionary ideal with a new one.

Israel failed to recognize the Messiah and the meaning of His mission. What of the new Israel which is God's people today? Archbishop Eugene D'Souza has already pointed out to the Fathers of the Second Vatican Council that less than five per cent of the Church's total endeavor in the world is presently committed to the realization of this mission among the peoples who have not yet heard even the name of their Redeemer— some two thirds of contemporary mankind.[1] It might seem that

[1] Vatican Council II, 5-E-63, October 4th: "If statistics are compiled of all the apostolic work which is done for the good of souls by priests and religious in the whole world, would not this be the result? By far the greatest part of the work—even in many of the territories of Propaganda

the Messianic Kingdom has been understood once again in terms of an everlasting kingdom on earth, not in Israel this time, but in Europe and the Americas. More than ninety per cent of the Church's visible membership, served by all but a fraction of her clergy and religious, are found in these lands; and it is two thousand years since Christ's final command to make disciples of *all* nations.[2] With only a handful of missionaries, functioning almost like the members of private clubs dedicated to works of supererogation on the outer fringes of the "Christian world," it might appear that the really serious business of the Church remains exclusively within the cultural sphere of ancient Christendom. And, with so many of the Christian missions abroad looking more like spiritual colonies of Europe than local flowerings from the seeds of faith, it might be suggested that these good works were actually intended to reflect more the glories of Christendom than of Christianity. In a word: Just how serious are we about being a *catholic* Church? Have we today even begun to appreciate what it means to be an essentially missionary Church, in the way that this notion has been expounded by the past four popes in their specific writings on this subject? Now if it is true that this notion, which has hardly been studied

---

Fide—is taken up with a pastoral program of conservation (I do not use the word pejoratively), that is, in preserving the faith and morals of Catholics. . . . Considerably less apostolic work is devoted to bringing back to the Church those who have fallen away. . . , in other words, to the sheep who have been lost of the House of Israel. But when we come to the immense mass of unbelievers, more than two billion pagans, they hardly receive the crumbs that fall from the table. Hardly five per cent, perhaps not even three per cent of the apostolic labors of the Church are devoted to them." "The Missionary Task of the Church," by Eugene D'Souza, Archbishop of Bhopal, India, *Council Speeches of Vatican II,* ed. by Yves Congar, Hans Küng, and Daniel O'Hanlon, Paulist Press, Glen Rock, N.J., 1964, pp. 281–282.

[2] Mt 28:19; Lk 24:47.

and only barely implemented, is "being erased with each passing day," then we have nearly reached the end of it. There really is not very much to be "erased."

And what does "the spiritual impregnation of the universe" mean to missionaries in Asia and Africa, and on the islands far away, where the Church has never even attempted to establish herself firmly and indigenously among the vast majority of the peoples? It is difficult to comment on this. But it does make one thing quite obvious. Missionaries in the field have remained silent far too long, while Christian writers in Europe and America have been fabricating their new theory of missionary activity. Unless these missionaries begin at least to ask a few pointed questions about all of this, the day may come very soon when they will be forced to ask themselves the practical question: "What are we doing here?" At least one member of the Council's Commission on the Missions contends that "the missions of the Church are not in Asia and Africa only; they are in New York, Chicago, Boston, London, Paris."[3] Let us translate this sentence into concrete terms. In the Archdiocese of Boston, there are more than two thousand priests serving a million and a half Catholics. In a much larger ecclesiastical jurisdiction in south-western Ethiopia, there are twenty priests trying to establish the Church among some four million non-Christians in a dozen or more distinct "tribes and tongues and peoples." If one of these priests were to leave Ethiopia and take up work in a Boston parish, would he be any less a missionary than he is now? In the new theory of the missions, the only difference would seem to be geographical. Have we really come this far?

[3] Fulton J. Sheen, *Worldmission,* 1963, vol. 14, no. 3, p. 12.

1. The Genesis and Significance of This New Concept

It seems to have started in France during and after the Second World War. This cataclysm forced all serious Christians to a radical reëvaluation of themselves. This collective examination of conscience was particularly searing in France and Belgium, with "the loss to the Church of the working class" as a kind of focal point, and as a challenge to the new self-awareness of the Christian remnant. The vigor of the Young Christian Worker movement and the earnestness of the Worker Priests were the outward signs of hope and of inner renewal. The Pentecostal spirit was in the air together with just enough political unrest and economic anxiety to produce a kind of explosive light, radiating even to the other parts of the Western world. French Catholic writers had, as they always have, a dramatic impact, captivating imaginations everywhere. We all recall Abbé Michonneau's *Revolution in a City Parish*. But perhaps it was Abbé Godin who raised the banner, and provided the marching song and the slogan, "France Pagan?", or "France a Mission Country!" And so the campaign has gone on, carrying this great issue before the eyes of the Christian world and right up the steps of St. Peter's into the aula. Now that this effort has been largely completed, and without in any way expressing the slightest doubt about the general validity of this renewal, it may be time to pause briefly and to examine quietly some of the suppositions on which it was based.

Just a few years ago, a very well known and articulate archbishop wrote a book on "missionary activity"—*The Gospel to Every Creature*,[4] which rarely mentions the work of establishing

[4] Kenedy, New York, 1957, by Leon Cardinal Suenens, Archbishop of Mechelen-Brussels.

the Church as an indigenous and self-sustaining entity among those distinctive ethnic-culture units of people that make up mankind: among the *gentes* of Scripture and the *ethnici* of the encyclical letters on the missions. Instead, the author seems to see "the missions" almost exclusively in terms of the apostasy and the leakage among "the masses" of Europe, where the existing parishes offer "an *unlimited* field of missionary activity" which is directed to "every single individual without exception in these parishes," and which "will *never be completed*." A French Dominican scholar has also given us another book on the same theme in his *A Mission Theology*.[5] This thoughtful and interesting work is profoundly concerned with the obligation of every Catholic in France to become a missionary in respect to all of the "lost sheep" within his own parish and his own milieu. But there is nothing said about the obligation of these same Catholics to participate in the Church's universal mission to the non-evangelized peoples who make up the vast majority of mankind. The concern of these books, and of so many other recent studies on the "missionary" problem, is not primarily for the completion of the Church's messianic mission of preaching the Gospel to every nation, and of establishing the Church for a witness among all the peoples of the world. Rather in these books the Church's missionary activity is given a new meaning, much broader than it has ever been before in theory, but necessarily somewhat narrower in practice.

Father Andrew Seumois, the dean of Catholic missiologists, tells us that among specialists in the field of mission theory there is widespread and "nearly unanimous agreement concerning the essential lines of definition for the missionary function" of the Church. But there is still "some problem outside of

[5] Notre Dame, 1962, by A. M. Henry, O.P.

missiological circles with language, particularly in France since 1943, with regard to the term 'mission'."[6] As a concrete example, he offers the following:

Attempts to confuse the concept of mission apostolate have been made by the journal *Parole et Mission* (Paris), which began in 1958 and is preoccupied with emphasizing a Theology of the Word especially directed toward the apostolate in the de-Christianized milieux of France.

This journal presents also some legitimate missionary articles, and then tries to force an analogy between the real mission countries and lands with a de-Christianized social milieu where the Church is still geographically implanted, making an identification of the two. It applies the wrong and vaguely analogical expression *"espaces humains"* to the situation of social milieux, thereby increasing the chance for confusion between the apostolate of social milieux and the proper missionary task. . . .[7]

The international review, *Christ to the World* (Rome), is another example of this tendency to confuse the two specifically different forms of apostolic work. In this case, it takes the form of a very consistent concern more with the *number* of individuals outside the visible Church than with the establishment of the Church indigenously among those for whom the Church has not yet existed in this way. In the words of the editor of this journal:

We are convinced that this widening of the notion of "mission" to comprise at the same time the apostolate among the pagans and the apostolate among the lost sheep, not only obviates all antagonism between missionary works and the interests of parish and diocesan works, but also promotes both of them. . . . We are working at Christ's work of redemption both in mission lands and in old Christian communities which have become at least to some extent mission

---

[6] "The Evolution of Mission Theology among Roman Catholics," by A. V. Seumois, O.M.I., *The Theology of the Christian Mission,* ed. by Gerald H. Anderson, C.S.M. Press, London, 1962, p. 130.

[7] *Ibid.,* p. 131.

lands again, because they contain *a large number* of men who do not know Christ and who are still far away from Him.[8]

Thus the conviction has been growing for some years in France, and has been rapidly spreading elsewhere, that missionary activity is equally concerned with searching out all of the sheep who have strayed from the existing flock in Europe and the Americas; and with so much emphasis having been given to the urgency of winning back the "de-Christianized masses," this form of the apostolate tends to assume priority over the other, especially as it is closer to home. How often have we heard it glibly said that the great problem of the Church today is "the loss of the workers"? But surely this is not "the problem" of the Church in North America, where there are more industrial workers than there are in France and Belgium combined. In fact, one may inquire whether it is *"the* problem" anywhere outside of those two countries.

In a more recent development of this new missionary outlook, many are thinking now of missionary activity primarily in terms of Latin America, where the social, economic, and pastoral problems are perhaps more acute than elsewhere—at least in their possible political significance. And therefore, more "missionaries" are needed in order "to stem the ominous trends toward sectarianism and Communism," as one North American bishop has phrased it,[9] perhaps also suggesting at the same time

[8] "The Apostolate of Non-Christians and De-Christianized People" by F. Legrand, *Missiology in Africa Today,* ed. by D. J. Hatton, Dublin, 1961, p. 137; italics added.

[9] Most Rev. K. J. Alter, *The Shield,* November 1962, vol. 42, no. 2, p. 3: "Unless extraordinary effort is made to save the situation, the Latin American countries, although Catholic in tradition, will succumb . . . to the danger of subversion, due to sectarian and Communist propaganda. . . . A positive effort of sufficient magnitude may not be too late to stem

the reasons for the current but rather late "missionary" interest in this area. Another member of the North American hierarchy has said that the distinction (which was explicitly made by Pius XI and retained in the documents and in the practice of the Church) between home and foreign missions is incorrect and misleading, as it distracts from the universal mission of the Church which is the same the world over: "to preach the Gospel to every creature in *every place—simultaneously—*until time will be no more."[10]

This spokesman for the new school of thought on this question is, therefore, quite consistent in his answer to the question, "What defines a mission territory?" "Only those places," he says, "in which *all* the inhabitants *believe in and practice* the faith, where there are *none* who are unacquainted with the Gospel and have *no need* of instruction—only of those territories can it be correctly stated that they are not mission countries."[11] If an order of priority is not clearly indicated, then it would follow that converting Baptists in Texas or searching for "lost sheep" in Dublin should be no different from the work of establishing the Church among Kenya's northern tribes who have never even heard the name of Christ, and for whom missionaries are not yet available. One of the unquestioned suppositions is that all apostolic works are on the same level of urgency. As most people probably assume that "charity begins at home," with "home" as the operative word, then the disproportion between the effort given to the care of Christian

---

the ominous trends in Latin America. If such an effort succeeds we may be able to unite all the American countries, both North and South, into a strong, cohesive defense in favor of Christian civilization."

[10] Most Rev. R. H. Ackerman, C.S.Sp., *The Shield,* November 1961, vol. 42, no. 2, p. 6; italics added.

[11] *Ibid.*

communities and the effort expended in establishing the Church among the peoples of Asia and Africa does not seem particularly alarming. In Europe—one notes, as a matter of interest—there is a general ratio of one priest for less than a thousand Catholics; and in France alone there are more priests and sisters than there are in the whole of Asia and Africa together. Even Latin America has a general ratio of one priest for every five thousand souls, as compared with one to seventeen thousand in Africa, and one to eighty thousand in Asia.

So nowadays, when people speak about the "renewal of the Pentecostal spirit" and the "essentially missionary nature of the Church," we must be circumspect; and when we are told, in the words of Cardinal Feltin, that "the whole Church must set itself in a state of missionary activity," we must be cautious. What these writers are primarily thinking about, more often than not, are the serious social and pastoral problems of the Church in parts of Europe and the Americas. And when one hears the new theology of the missions being expounded, if he listens carefully, he will recognize that these theories are concerned almost exclusively with what most Anglo-Saxons still call "pastoral theology." By using the words "mission" and "missionary" in relation to whatever particular problem happens to appear most urgent to them, Catholic writers have engendered some considerable confusion; and invariably, they have lost sight of the precise aims of missionary activity as formulated in the official documents of the Church. By confusing the "de-Christianized" social milieux of Europe and the Americas with the non-evangelized *gentes* of the rest of the world, it should become possible, in this new orientation of the Church's missionary function, to intensify "missionary zeal" while at the same time demanding no more sacrifices than are presently being made for the extension of the

Church among the peoples of the non-Western world. The result is that, in good conscience, the Church may remain primarily an affair of Europe and the Americas. The proper care of the existing flock is surely capable of absorbing more and more of those missionary resources which even now amount to little more than a parsimonious token.

With all of this very earnest and often profound concern over the mission of the Church in the modern Western world, there sometimes seems to be almost a tacit assumption that the Church is already known and accessible throughout the rest of the world. And therefore, it is concluded, all that remains is to intensify our zeal in watching over the existing flock; and, while gathering in as many as possible of the lost sheep, to prepare for the attacks of the Antichrist (usually Communism), as we await the conversion of the Jews and the return of the Lord. In this conception, the Church's pastoral functions, home missions, social action, university students, workers, poor peasants, blind intellectuals, old folks, orphans, etc., may all be regarded as the proper objects of "missionary activity."

Even in the missions of Asia and Africa, there is this strong tendency to permit the present limited missionary resources to be absorbed almost exclusively in fields where the good seed has already been sown once. Among missionaries in India, this has come to be known as the "choke-law." The successful evangelization of large numbers of people in one or another region, especially when this achievement is coupled with a chronic shortage of personnel, is apt to result in the total stagnation of missionary expansion among the remaining non-evangelized peoples. So many missionaries are taken up with the pastoral care of the converted that further expansion is "choked." This problem was dealt with in a special instruction from Rome to the Bishops of

29

India, "not just exhorting . . . but positively enjoining" that new mission stations be established among those not yet evangelized, and that each bishop should make available exclusively for this work at least two missionaries, with the names of these missionaries being sent to Rome within six months after the reception of the instruction.[12] This was in 1893. In his report on the work of evangelization in India, submitted to the Episcopal Conference of India in 1951, Bishop William Bouter had once again to bring up the old question of "stagnation and absorption in parochial duties to the exclusion of work *'ad paganos'* [the "choke-law"] . . . owing to insufficiency of personnel."[13] Thus the failure to understand the urgent nature and the specific goals of missionary activity is not confined to Europe and the Americas only.

Any confusion on the meaning of the Church's missionary function is bound to lead to disastrous conclusions, even if such are not intended. Some of these conclusions can be foreseen as inevitable. According to a missiologist who has made a special study of the various connotations of the words "mission" and "missionary," this is what has happened as a result of the attempt to apply these words to the ecclesiastical activity undertaken in the "de-Christianized" regions of Europe:

It should be noted that this has had unhealthy results among French youth, for the idea sprung up that the needs of the Church in France were of a "missionary" nature, were in fact so urgent that it was both unpatriotic and un-Christian to abandon the "mission fields of France" for apostolic labor in foreign fields. This resulted in a certain loss of interest in the foreign mission apostolate—and this in a country which was a leader in Europe in promoting foreign missions.[14]

[12] *Cum Postremis, S. Congr. Prop. Fide,* March 19th, 1893; *Christ to the World,* 1960, vol. 5, no. 2, p. 236.

[13] *Christ to the World,* 1959, vol. 1, no. 6, p. 50.

[14] *Mission and Missions,* an unpublished paper by Ronan Hoffman, O.F.M. Conv., S.T.D., The Catholic University of America.

Certainly, the whole Church has not gone this far, nor will she. But how can we explain such a tendency which is undeniably present? Perhaps we might think of it in terms of an admittedly far-fetched analogy. If all of the most articulate writers in the medical field were members of a certain school of thought in the United States, and were profoundly influenced by their experience with one presumably great modern American medical problem, the rest of us—reading their works for ten or twenty years— might eventually come to believe that the major threat to world health today is obesity. At least, we might find it difficult to believe that, in fact, the major threat is just the opposite—in the much larger world outside of America. Has something like this happened in our thinking about the mission of the Church in the modern world?

Among the African peoples living south of the Sahara, the Catholic population has almost doubled since 1949. Yet the faithful here represent only about ten per cent of the total population; and the number of priests working in these areas has increased by only fifty-nine per cent since 1949.[15] Because this precarious situation was foreseen, Pius XII himself in 1952 made a special appeal to the universal Church, pleading for more priests to be sent to Africa "before it is too late." The Pope was not concerned merely with bridging the ever-widening gap between the rapidly increasing number of the faithful and the number of priests required for their pastoral care. He was equally anxious to forestall the inexorable "choke-law" with respect to the vast majority of the pagan peoples who have not yet heard the good news of the Gospel in this most fruitful mission field of the Church's long history. Even the tone of this encyclical letter was extraordinarily urgent and moving: "There is cause for grave concern

[15] *Herder Correspondence*, February 1964, vol. 1, no. 2, pp. 37–38.

in this . . . Will the sons of the Church understand their duty . . .?"

In one particular place there are forty priests for almost a million souls. . . . In another place, there are fifty priests for a population of two million inhabitants, while the sixty thousand faithful would be enough to absorb all the time of the missionaries.

. . . Twenty more priests in a particular region would make it possible to plant the cross there today, while tomorrow this same land, tilled by workers other than those of the Lord, will have probably become impervious to the true faith.[16]

For all his pleading, and in spite of his urgent tone, the results of the Pope's appeal were disappointing. Fewer than three hundred priests were sent to Africa in response to this request.[17] This was about one quarter of the actual number needed merely to meet the emergency pastoral situation. Subsequently, and as a matter of policy in Ruanda, missionaries had to desist from further evangelization in the fields which are ripe for the harvest.[18] Yet, on the other hand, there are more than five thousand priests in French schools, for the most part teaching merely secular subjects.[19] One school alone in Brussels has on its faculty more priests than the entire city of Leopoldville in The Congo; and there are seminaries in Switzerland with an average of one priest for every two students.[20] While there are historical explanations, and perhaps even justifying reasons, for such a disproportionate distribution of the Church's personnel, the over-

[16] *Fidei Donum,* by Pope Pius XII, *AAS,* 1952, p. 370; tr. NCWC, nos. 28–36. On October 18th, 1964, Pope Paul VI asked the dioceses and religious orders of Europe and America to do *now* for Africa what they have done for Latin America.

[17] *Herder Correspondence, loc. cit.*

[18] *Missions in the World Today,* by René P. Millot, Hawthorn, New York, 1961, p. 98.

[19] *Christ to the World,* 1961, vol. 6, no. 1, p. 27.

[20] *Ibid.*

all picture suggested through these figures is alarming when considered in relation to the Church's universal mission. It is estimated that in all of our so-called "foreign missions," there are hardly more than one thousand priests (out of a total of nearly four hundred thousand in the whole world) working exclusively or mainly among the peoples who have not yet heard the Gospel message.[21] The remaining priests in these same lands, embracing almost two-thirds of mankind today, number only some thirty thousand and are almost exclusively absorbed in the care of Christian communities; moreover, even to cope with this pastoral and social work of the Church, their number is hopelessly inadequate in most regions. It is obvious what this must mean in terms of the evangelization of new peoples.

2. The Words

Obviously, much of the confusion being propagated though the new concept of missionary activity is due to the limited choice of words we have when we wish to present, with dramatic impact, an urgent problem. Alas for the poverty of human language! "With these few words," wrote Father Karl Rahner, "the whole immense reality of the divine order of salvation has to be expressed, and it has to be referred to again and again, briefly, without long explanations. Consequently, we will always have too few words and too many things to be named."[22] Still, we might wonder just why "missionary activity" should have been chosen as the means of dramatizing the urgent need for adapting the pastoral and social functions of the Church to the new conditions in

[21] *Ibid.*, and no. 2, p. 151.

[22] *Mary, Mother of the Lord,* by Karl Rahner, S.J., Herder and Herder, New York, 1963, p. 95.

parts of Europe and the Americas. We have already seen how little urgency, in practice, is attached to these words when used in their traditional sense. Perhaps it was only their romantic and challenging connotations which made these terms attractive and useful. Among the more superficial, it was perhaps the "useful-gimmick" attitude toward the missions: a kind of exploitation similar to what we may observe, for example, in the vocation-recruitment and fund-raising practices of certain "missionary" societies which actually send overseas merely a fraction of their personnel, and only a token of the donations solicited in the name of their missions—practices sadly reminiscent of the sin of Ananias and Sapphira, who suffered death for their fraud of holding back part of the free offerings. Is it too much to call things by their names? We are, after all, in the "latter days" of this world.

On the other hand, there is profound theological and historical meaning in the words "mission" and "missionary." It is quite valid to speak of the Church's mission in the world, realizing that this does not refer merely to foreign missionary actvity, but includes also pastoral and social action in lands where the Church has been established already on firm foundations. But some care must be taken to avoid confusion. Guided by Father Ronan Hoffman's work to which we referred a few pages back, it is possible to untangle the various meanings of these key words.

The denotation of the word "mission" is concerned simply with "sending." Thus, the general connotation in Christian tradition has been one of "sending" apostolic workers to preach the Gospel away from their "homeland," or among peoples other than those who sent them. Such is the meaning of the word "apostle" in the New Testament. It was the Lord Himself who first chose to designate the twelve with this precise name[23] borrowed from

[23] Lk 6:13.

34

Hebrew legal terminology, where "*shaliah*" had, and still has, the specific meaning of one who is sent abroad to function as a legal agent of the sender whose authority he represents and in whose name he acts. This implication of "sending" or "being sent" abroad, away from the place of origin, is essential to the Christian notion of apostleship, which is a participation in the messianic mission of the Son: "As the Father sent me, so I send you."[24] For this "grace of apostleship" is given "in order to bring about obedience to faith among the nations."[25]

The apostles were, of course, the first Christian missionaries sent abroad to peoples other than their own; and all of their successors are, in the words of Pius XII, "the envoys and missionaries of the Lord par excellence."[26] And here the Pope makes a clear distinction between pastoral and missionary duties:

If every bishop is the proper pastor of that portion of the flock entrusted to his care, his quality as a legitimate successor of the apostles by divine institution renders him jointly responsible for the apostolic mission of the Church. . . .[27]

The responsibility of each bishop for the Church's missions abroad is, therefore, on a level of "equality" with his pastoral duty toward that particular portion of the flock entrusted to his care:[28] "For I do not mean that the relief of others should become your burden, but that there should be equality."[29] Not only the bishops, but all of the faithful as well are charged with this catholic responsibility. "This is so to such an extent," wrote Pius XII, "that a Christian is not truly faithful and devoted to the Church if he is not *equally* attached and devoted to her uni-

[24] Jn 20:21.   [25] Rom 1:5.
[26] *Op. cit.,* no. 60.   [27] *Ibid.,* no. 59.
[28] *Ibid.,* no. 95.   [29] 2 Cor 8:13.

versality, desiring that she take root and flourish in all parts of the earth."[30] This aspect of the mission of the Son, extended through all the bishops to all of the peoples who still await the advent of the Messiah, has not been dwelled on by theologians who, through the centuries, have tended to limit their use of the word "mission" to their discussions on the processions within the Holy Trinity. But theologians nowadays are giving much more attention to the matter as they explore more and more the implications of episcopal collegiality.

Canon Law gives a number of meanings to the word "mission." It may mean empowering someone to exercise jurisdiction. It may also signify the granting of authority to preach, either to the faithful (internal) or to non-believers (external). The relevant meaning in relation to the present discussion is limited, both in the singular and in the plural, to the territories under the direction of the Sacred Congregation de Propaganda Fide. It must, of course, be recognized that true missionary activity in the traditional sense is also carried on in certain other territories which, for historical or political reasons, do not fall into this canonical category—as, for example, Angola and Mozambique. Therefore, Canon Law does not prove a point one way or the other; it is merely evidence for a particular use of the word in the practice and in the organization of the Church. What is of more immediate interest to our question is the historical usage.

During the patristic and scholastic periods, the word "mission" was generally taken only in the juridical sense of an authoritative sending to preach, while retaining also the theological meaning in reference to the inner life of the Trinity. It was the Jesuits of the sixteenth century who gave the word its special meaning in connection with the evangelization of infidels in foreign lands,

[30] *Op. cit.,* no. 62.

36

using it also to refer to the journeys to and from these distant places. By the end of the seventeenth century, the generally accepted meaning (aside from the ingrained theological terms) referred always and exclusively to foreign missions, or to the apostolate among the non-evangelized peoples outside of Europe —thus also excluding Protestant Christians.[31a] This connotation has been generally retained up to the present time in the minds of the faithful, in the official documents, and in the practice of the Church. This is exemplified especially in the five encyclical letters treating specifically of the missions, in the orientation of the pontifical mission aid societies, and in the work of the Sacred Congregation de Propaganda Fide. It would, therefore, seem fair to conclude that this special meaning of "missionary activity," after four centuries of such general usage, has become traditional.

All of this should not preclude the possibility, and indeed the urgent necessity, of further discussion aimed at deepening and even broadening our understanding of missionary activity. The traditional concept needs to be radically reconsidered in the light of modern world problems. But, in seeking to renew the missionary spirit, we cannot afford to ignore all that this has meant to the Church up to now. This is our only valid starting point.

3. The Functions

We might take this whole discussion out of the realm of semantics for a moment, and, without the conventional terms which have now become questionable, consider merely the basic realities involved. These realities are as follows. The Church has an

[31a] This is confirmed in the *Dogmatic Constitution on the Church,* where "the missions" are regarded only with respect to non-Christians (II, 15–16).

37

eschatological work to do in the world. Primarily, this consists in making Christ sacramentally present to all men, by preaching the Gospel to all nations and establishing the Church among each people for a witness before the whole world. The Church, as a mystical and at the same time tangible body of believing witnesses, is more than just a means of salvation. The Church is Christ sacramentally bringing salvation to visibly and corporately signified realization among the distinctive ethnic-culture units of people who make up mankind. For she is, according to the words of the First Vatican Council, "the sign raised up (*signum levatum*) among the nations, inviting all who have *not yet* believed."[31] And the Council refers us to the messianic prophecy of Isaiah: ". . . a signal beckoning to the peoples all around . . . high lifted up for a world to see it, the standard that shall call Israel home, gather in the exiled sons of Juda from the four corners of the earth."[32] As the Bible teaches, it is by this sign that they are called out of every nation, the chosen witnesses together with the cultural wealth of all the nations; back to Jerusalem renewed they come flocking, watched over by faithful pastors of the Lord's own choosing. Thus, the deliverer makes good His promise through the historical extension of the Church in different times and places among the nations; thus He holds assize upon all peoples and races, that His glory may be revealed to all and His mark set upon each one of them. And what of those chosen witnesses whose deliverance has already been signified to them through their membership in the Church raised up among them on firm and indigenous foundations?

I have an errand for them, to be my messengers across the sea; to Africa and to Lydia where men draw the bow, . . . and to the islands far away.

[31] Vatican Council I, *DB.*, no. 1794.   [32] Is 11:10–12.

They shall go out where men never heard of my name, never saw my glory yet, to reveal that glory among the nations.

And out of all the nations they shall bring your brethren back. . . . And some among these newcomers, the Lord says, I will choose out to be priests and Levites.[33]

Is this not a true notion of the Church and the essential meaning of the Christian vocation of universal witness in the dimensions of historical time and place? And does this not entail two obvious and equally essential functions through which the Church is to become historically, and in the sight of all men, what she is: the New Israel?

The first of these two functions is prior in both the order of time and of urgency. This consists in the activity of raising up the sign of salvation among a people who have not yet believed. Consequently, the second function consists in the activity of maintaining the clarity of this sign once it has been raised up among a people, so that it will be something meaningful and salutary for all who live in the nation. Then again, the first function becomes a consequence of the second, which continues to exist primarily for the sake of raising up this sign among more and more new peoples among whom Christ has not yet become sacramentally present through the Church firmly established among them. Each of these two activities finds its completion in the other, mutually signifying the eschatological nature and aims of the Church in history. For the Church on earth will have fulfilled her vocation, and human history will have been completed, once this sign has been raised up among all peoples for a witness, signifying sacramentally to the whole world the deliverance of mankind, accomplished "once for all"[34] through the Messiah. The Church is truly herself and actually alive to the extent that

[33] Is 66:18–21.   [34] Heb 7:27; 9:26–28.

she is striving to be, in historical tangibility, the sacramental *Lumen Gentium*.

Up to now, the first of the two functions just indicated has been traditionally called "missionary activity"; the second function has been understood as "pastoral activity." If we wish now to modify the connotations of these words, then we must be careful to understand the precise nature of the distinctive functions signified, and we must find other appropriate terms for expressing the actual and concrete realities. What is important is not the words, but the specific functions which must somehow be clearly understood and designated. Therefore, for example, we might say that the Church has one mission in the world, and this one mission is historically worked out through two different, although mutually dependent, functions. One of these basic activities is primarily, but not exclusively, concerned with gathering a flock which does not yet exist, or extending the Church to more and more new peoples. The other is primarily, but not exclusively, concerned with watching over the health and the increase of the already existing flock, or the pastoral and social care of the faithful already gathered around the visible Church in their own nation. When thus understood, the two functions may be seen as manifestations of the one mission of the Church in action.

According to Seumois, the general opinion of Catholic missiologists is

. . . that mission activity is a specific task, quite distinct, in the ecclesiastical ministry. . . . The ordinary ecclesiastical ministry is twofold: *pastoral* (for the care of the faithful in the Church), and *apostolic* (for the conversion to the Church).

Many kinds of apostolate can be distinguished, but missionary activity is a specific field of the apostolate aimed at bringing the Church to souls where she is not yet established, in order to bring souls to the Church, i.e., implanting the Church in a new area so that a new particular (regional) church may be set up, live, and grow in an autochthonous way by her own personnel and means.[35]

And once this "regional" Church has been so established among a particular people, it must in turn send out missionaries to other non-evangelized peoples; for this is its historical *raison d'être* in the eschatological economy of mankind's redemption; and this is the condition for its own vital growth: "Their own growth in holiness will be in proportion to their active interest in the holy missions."[36] Here, it should be noted, Pius XII was speaking of "missions" in the traditional sense.

No matter what words we may use, one thing is certain. Both the pastoral and the missionary functions of the Church are equally essential to the life of the whole Church everywhere; and the mission of the Church is not being served where one or the other of these activities is being neglected in practice. Where the apostolic zeal of the Christian community—whether in Europe, the Americas, Asia, Africa, or Oceania—is primarily turned inward, defensively on itself, and not equally turned outward in a truly catholic attitude of world-wide dimensions, there the faith is bound to wither and to die. This is the most disturbing aspect of the new concept which, as we have seen, tends to focus apostolic zeal on the peoples among whom the Church already exists in at least some historically tangible way, while hardly mentioning the others to whom the Church has never been made known and accessible in terms of their own concrete history.

It would be enlightening to study the reasons why the Church in parts of Europe and the Americas has fallen back into a condition resembling that of mission territories. Doubtless, the

---

[35] *Loc. cit.*

[36] *Evangelii Praecones,* by Pope Pius XII, *AAS,* 1951, p. 507; tr. C. McAuliffe, S.J., America Press, New York, 1957, no. 101.

historical causes would be very complex and peculiar to the respective regions. We would want to know the answers to Christopher Dawson's searching questions: What was it that spread; by what process; and by what character of men?[37] Perhaps it might even be found that among some of these peoples true evangelization never occurred, that the Church had never really been firmly established among them on indigenous foundations. Then, of course, these peoples would still be the proper objects of the Church's missionary activity. But it might also be found that some, for whom the Church once existed as a vital reality, were subsequently faithless to their Christian calling with regard to other non-evangelized peoples; thus, the faith which was not communicated to others has been lost. Would such people once again become the proper objects of the Church's missionary solicitude? Are the fields in which the good seed has already been sown once to be plowed up and sown over again, while the seed has not yet been sown even once in other fields? The Lord of the harvest said that the field in which the good seed has already been sown once is to be left until the reapers appear at the end of the world.[38]

The missionary activity of planting the seeds of faith among the nations is an eschatological function of the Church, moving

[37] "In reading the history of the geographical expansion of Christianity, we cannot be satisfied with quantitative standards. At every stage we are faced with the problem of quality, with the nature of the religion which is diffused and the character of the men who are diffusing it. At every stage we must ask, what is it that spread? What effect did it have on its environment and vice versa? And why has the process of expansion sometimes been arrested or reversed? But it is not easy to answer these questions." "The Expansion of Christianity," by Christopher Dawson, *The Commonweal,* January 9th, 1959, vol. 69, no. 5, p. 379.

[38] Mt 13:24–43.

through time and place with the irreversible and unrepeatable nature of all historical events. The peoples among whom the Church once existed, but is now no longer visibly present, are not worse off than those for whom the Church has not yet been present once. There is nothing in Scripture about "reëvangelization." The Gospel must *first* be preached for a witness among every people, and *then* shall the end come.[39] There is no promise that once the visible Church has taken root among a particular people, it will then remain there for ever. The process is eschatological. The end must come some time.

Certainly, the "apostasy of the masses" in parts of Europe is a matter of vital concern to the whole Church, as also are the poverty, ignorance, and exploitation of the faithful in parts of Latin America. The whole Body suffers with each member. Generous help is needed, therefore, to fill the fissures in some of the archaic and rapidly crumbling social structures. Indeed, a total Christian renewal of the whole structure is required in some places, lest it be refashioned by Communism. Many sacrifices must be made in order to supply more priests for Christian communities which now have no pastors. But where are these sacrifices to be suffered? Are more missionaries now to be sent to these communities instead of to the peoples who have not yet been evangelized once? An affirmative answer to the question is generally implied in the new concept of missionary activity. But can we truly ransom the times and serve our universal mission by cutting back, in effect, on our already scanty missionary commitments elsewhere in order to make a concentrated, eleventh-hour stand inside the tottering citadels of ancient Christendom?

Paul VI was still using the traditional meaning of "mission-

[39] Mk 13:10; Mt 24:14.

ary" when he addressed the Pontifical Commission on Latin America and the Latin American Bishops' Council on July 9th, 1963. He said then that the problem of the Church in the particular regions of Latin America is essentially a matter of "more intensive pastoral action" and socio-economic action "which is not directly the mission of the Church." It would seem to be a matter of missionary action as such, only in respect to the various aboriginal tribes who still—after centuries of Hispanic Christianity in Latin America—have not yet been evangelized once. This brings us back to the traditional notion of missionary activity as something quite distinct from the pastoral care of the existing flock.

4. The Distinction of Functions

Between surgeons there are differences of technique and of method in performing operations; but they all have the same final aim of alleviating human suffering and of curing their patients; and they all seek to achieve this aim through the specific activity of surgery. Medical doctors pursue this same final aim, but in a specifically different way: through the use of medicines, which, however, may be administered by various techniques and methods—by means of injection, for example, or in the form of capsules. Both surgeons and medical doctors are engaged in the same *kind* of work. Their methods and techniques are what differ. But even more than this, the actual approach of a surgeon to his patient is specifically different from that of a medical doctor. In terms of action, in the organization and orientation of his daily task, each is determined by immediate goals and by guiding principles which are more than differences in technique and method. Their mediate aims are of the same *kind*, but their immediate goals are of different *species.* So their respective activities are *specifically different,* although they are mutually dependent and complementary because of the same general aim and orientation with respect to the patients. This is the sort of relationship that pertains between missionary activity and pastoral activity. Both missionaries and pastors have the same final aim with respect to the people they have been called to serve. But their respective functions differ in more than technique and method only.

The work of raising up a sign for the first time among a people, and the effort of adapting this sign so that it will be truly intelligible in its new cultural context, is not the same as the work of those who must subsequently strive to maintain the intelligibility of the sign in the gradually changing cultural context of their own people. Trying to gather together a flock which does not yet exist is not the same thing as caring for the health and the natural increase of an already existing flock. One is a convocation; the other is a congregation. They are mutually dependent and intrinsically related to one another. Were they not, there would be no need to make and maintain the distinction. Both of these functions are equally essential to the life of the whole Church everywhere. Missionary activity terminates in pastoral activity, which, in turn, generates further missionary activity. The vitality of one increases or decreases with the vitality of the other. It is like the essential relationship between prayer and apostolic action: One could not be what it is without the other. But in terms of their immediate goals, they are *specifically different.*

This distinction of functions has been explicitly maintained in the practice of the Church during the past four hundred years, at least. But it is actually much older. For is this not the very same distinction made by St. Paul both in his writings and in the conduct of his own life? "Some He has appointed to be apostles, others to be prophets, others to be evangelists, or pastors, or teachers, for the sake of ordering the lives of the faithful ... and building up the frame of Christ's body ... no longer driven before the winds of each new doctrine ... to the functioning in due measure of each single part. . . ."[40] More than five hundred brethren witnessed the glorified Christ without all thereby being called to apostleship. Paul himself, called not as a pastor but as a missionary to the nations,[41] had even to vindicate his appointment to apostleship,[42] which is given in order to bring about obedience to faith among the nations[43]—and not for preaching "this Gospel where Christ has already been named."[44]

Dare we jettison all of this, now to be driven before the winds of a new doctrine? Do we really need an entirely new theory of missionary activity which finds its starting point not in Scripture and tradition, but in the socio-economic and pastoral problems of the Church in parts of Europe and the Americas? Some of these very problems are perhaps due to a general failure to take seriously the traditional concept of missionary activity by applying this notion extensively with all of the generous sacrifices it demands. Has this missionary function of the Church been given its due measure for the building up of the frame of Christ's Body? Belloc, speaking the mind of his time, said that "Europe is the faith. The faith is Europe."[45] We know better now. So perhaps it is time also to face the thought that the

40 Eph 4:11–16.   41 1 Cor 1:17; 3:10.
42 Gal 1:1, 15–17; 2:6–10; Eph 3:7–13.
43 Rom 1:5; 15:18.
44 Rom 15:20–21; 1 Cor 1:17; Acts 13:2; 26:17–18.
45 *Europe and the Faith,* by H. Belloc, London, 1920, p. 331.

Church, who is destined to grow among more and more new peoples, may at the same time even cease to exist visibly among some of her older peoples. Have some of them already reached the end of the "latter days" of the eschatological process, when the wickedness of men increases and charity grows cold, and even the elect may be deceived? The fields in which the good seed has already been planted are to be left to the care of their own husbandmen until all the other fields have been sown, so that the reaping of all shall be done at the end, at that end when some of the first will be last and the last will be first. From the viewpoint of mankind's corporate salvation, neither the first nor the last are any better or worse off than the other. From the missionary viewpoint, the present problems of some of the first to have been evangelized cannot be given priority over the last who have not yet been evangelized once. We know of no promise that the Church will remain forever where she has once existed visibly, and no command that we should "reëvangelize" those for whom the sign of salvation has already been raised up. But we do know that the Church must come into visible existence among the peoples who have not yet seen the *Lumen Gentium* established within their tangible history on firm and indigenous foundations, and that the final command of the Lord is concerned specifically and primarily with such peoples.

II.

Missionary Aims

The apostolic spirit consists rather in extending the frontiers of the Church than in perfecting a small part.

FRANCIS LIBERMANN

Is the missionary task of the Church, assigned to all Christians by the final command of the Lord, capable of completion? There is, as we have seen, a widespread assumption that the visible Church on earth is destined somehow and sometime to become numerically conterminous with all of the inhabitants living on the earth, so that, as a consequence, "missionary activity" is simultaneously directed to the termination of unbelief anywhere and everywhere, at home as well as abroad; for a mission territory is any place where at least one person is unacquainted with the Gospel, or needing instruction, or not living according to the principles of his faith in Christ. On this supposition, it may be, and is frequently, urged that more missionaries should be sent abroad because there are more infidels to be converted in Asia and Africa and Oceania than there are Christians to be served, and lost sheep to be found, in Europe and the Americas. This kind of quantitative thinking leans heavily on what we might call "the argument from numbers." And it is invariably supported by a questionable translation, which is then taken in a numerically literal sense, of the missionary mandate contained in the Gospel according to St. Mark, where the Greek sense is not "every creature" in individual computability, but "all creation" in its totality.[1]

1. Quantitative or Symbolic Goals?

If we ignore the notion of mankind's corporate salvation;[2] if we do not take account of the other formulations of, and references to, the missionary mandate;[3] if we forget what St. Paul said about the deliverance of "creation itself,"[4] and what St. Peter and St. John thought about the "new heaven and the new earth,"[5] then it becomes easy for us to see the goals of missionary activity in the simple terms of converting to visible membership in the Church every single individual on earth, taken in a numerical and quantitative sense. Therefore, our missionary activity may be carried on anywhere and everywhere simultaneously, without any clearly defined order of priority; for the end is not in sight anyway, the fields are all "unlimited," and the work "will never be completed." We have already considered some of the novel implications of this particular orientation of the Church's missionary function. Now we must question the underlying, and not very new, "argument from numbers."

Assuming that the goal of Catholic missionary activity were the visible conversion to the Church of every single person on earth, presumably then at some very future date all men will be simultaneously and tangibly within the fold, and then shall the Lord return in glory. What are the prospects for such an achievement? Where are the grounds for hope? It is a datum

---

[1] Mk 16:15.   [2] See Chapter 4.
[3] Mt 24:14; 28:19; Mk 13:10; Lk 24:47.
[4] Rom 8:18–22.   [5] 2 Pt 3:13; Ap 21:1, 22–27.

of history that the vast majority of redeemed mankind has so far remained outside the visible Church. Indeed, this majority never even hear of her while they are on earth. And what of most of our contemporaries living today in this latter half of the twentieth century after Christ? Are we moving toward or away from this goal of total membership in the visible Church? It would seem obvious that we are moving progressively backward. The number of Christians in the world is actually becoming fewer each year in relation to the total number of inhabitants on our planet. With human populations multiplying ever more rapidly everywhere, but most especially in lands where the Church does not exist and where populations are expected to double within the next twenty-five years, we can take little comfort from the statistics of our baptismal registers. Besides, the religion of Islam is increasing today by at least four new believers to every new Christian. Even if we were able to double our present rate of converting individuals everywhere in the world, where would we be in terms of numbers? The gap is growing ever wider, so our measurable achievements must become annually more futile in respect to such an impossible goal. And would not our hopes for the final coming of the Lord become even dimmer than they are now? We might even be tempted, in spite of what Scripture tells us repeatedly about missionary activity being *completed* among one people after another, to say that Christ has commanded us to an impossible task which cannot be completed. Will the end never come?

The achievement of the Church's missionary aims, and indeed the final fulfillment of her earthly mission, is not measured by the number of Christians in the world versus the number of non-Christians. The accomplishment of the missionary function among the nations is a conditional *sign* of the end.[6] The presence of the Church among the nations is a sacramental, and therefore symbolic, sign which tangibly signifies an invisible reality. Precisely because it is a symbolic sign, its validity does not depend on the total conversion to the visible Church of every single individual in one place; for only a few are chosen to stand for the whole of mankind; only a few are chosen to stand for all among their own people. Nor does the validity of this sign depend on the historical perseverance of the visible Church among one particular people; for it is not an everlasting kingdom anywhere on this earth—a truth which is also symbolized by the precarious existence, in different times and places, of the Church who is, in this historical aspect, an earthen vessel as fragile as the men whose faith makes her significant in the histories of their own peoples. Even in the last days, after the Gospel shall have been preached for a witness among all peoples, there will still remain countless non-believers, as charity grows cold and the wickedness of men increases, and even some of the elect may be deceived.[7] "When the Son of Man comes, will He find, do you think, faith on earth?"[8] The visible Church of explicit faith can never be conterminous with mankind in a numerically quantitative sense. The pursuit of such a goal would be a futile dissipation of our catholic energies which contribute to the expansion of the Church, even statistically in the long run, only when concentrated on their proper objectives.

Doubtless, most societies of missionaries have, at one time or another, gone through a period of sharp debate on this subject. By the very nature of their activity in the field, missionaries are forced to ask themselves just what it is they are trying to achieve. There were those zealous missionaries who believed—many of them still do—that all available resources should be directly brought to bear on the immediate conversion of the greatest possible number of individuals among whatever peoples happen to appear more responsive than others. In the opposite camp, missionaries have argued, with a notable measure of success and official support, for a more systematic organization of missionary activity, with the available personnel spread out more thinly to cover even the less tractable populations, and with more emphasis on the long-term work of social action and formal education aimed at the eventual training of a local clergy and the formation of an articulate Christian community. We may recall some of the stormy episodes, not so far back in mission history, when "innovators" such as Bishop Shanahan in Africa and Père Lebbe in China forced the issues into the open and won their point. This question was settled (at least in theory) among the Holy Ghost Fathers more than one hundred years ago. As Superior General of this missionary congregation, Father Libermann's aim in the missions of Africa was to produce something stable and lasting through the formation of a native clergy "rooted in the country." To those who disagreed with his decision in favor of diffusing the available resources and of giving priority to long-term planning, he would reply:

Do not forget that you are there not for the present, but to build for the future. . . . Ten souls you save by a hurried and ill-conceived step, by a measure which produces immediate good results, may perhaps mean the loss of more than a hundred thousand. . . . The apostolic spirit consists rather in extending the frontiers of the Church than in perfecting a small part.

[9] Quoted by H. J. Koren, C.S.Sp., *The Spiritans,* Duquesne, Pittsburgh, 1958, pp. 166, 170.

Formulations

The Jesuit Father Pierre Charles, who has probably done more than any other single person to clarify the meaning of missionary activity, has often been criticized for saying that "the missionary is not charged to save souls, but to install the visible Church where it did not exist before."[10] This proposition, taken without reference to its total context, is particularly disturbing to those who see missionary work primarily in terms of snatching as many individuals as possible from the dominion of Satan, from superstition, savagery, or the worship of idols. Nor is this formula pleasing to those who conceive the missionary task as an unending effort to terminate unbelief anywhere and everywhere simultaneously.

Theologically, it is quite sound to say that the missionary is not directly and primarily concerned with saving souls, but with founding the visible Church among people. Our very notion of "souls" is relevant only in reference to "persons" who exist only in community; and no man, whether priest or bishop or pope, "saves" other men. Salvation is God's work, accomplished by Christ and sacramentally signified through the Church's indigenous presence among peoples.

The visible Church, firmly established among a people, is the sacramental or mystical Christ doing among this people what historically He has already *done once for all who await Him*.[11] This unique saving event happened among one particular people at one precise place and time in mankind's history. But this event is "for all." Therefore, the historical work of the redeem-

10 *Worldmission,* 1960, vol. 11, no. 4, p. 9.
11 Heb 9:26–28

ing Christ is sacramentally extended, in other times and places, to more and more particular peoples, through the visible Church firmly established among them, thus gradually bringing to sacramentally signified completion, in the sight and in the hearing of all men, the one salutary work already accomplished historically by Christ for all mankind. It is through the efforts and the witness of missionaries, establishing the Church among the nations who have not yet known Christ, that the one messianic mission is being progressively achieved, that the history of man's salvation is being fulfilled and the way prepared for the coming of the Lord.

Because of the spatio-temporal condition of all men, God's saving will was actually accomplished by Christ in the real history and in the true flesh of men. For the same reason, this accomplishment continues sacramentally in the dimensions of "biological space-time," to use a very apt expression borrowed from Teilhard de Chardin; for what is essentially involved is the whole human condition: the biological continuity, the cultural genius, and the total history of all the distinctive ethnic-culture units of people who are mankind in the totality of past, present, and future, with all of their free actions constituting the history of salvation. Thus, missionary activity is essentially eschatological. It consists in making Christ sacramentally present, once for all, to those who await Him in faith, within the limited history and circumscribed culture of each biological family (uniting past and future in ethnic unity), through the establishment of the visible Church as an indigenously incarnated and self-sustaining entity among every people. All of this leads to one thing for which the Church exists and for which all Christians pray daily: the advent of the Lord and His messianic Kingdom. "Come Lord Jesus." "Thy kingdom come."

Abbot Vonier has further clarified the thought of Pierre Charles in relation to the alleged dichotomy between "saving souls" and "establishing the Church":

We may say that the true formula for Catholic missionary zeal is this: to plant the Church where it has not been before. If we read the Acts of the Apostles carefully, we shall certainly be convinced that apostolic activity was essentially directed to the foundation of churches everywhere. . . . The conquest of the individual soul seems to be subordinate to the vaster scheme of establishing the Church; it would be a very incomplete concept of Catholic activity in the mission field to think only of the salvation of individuals: such is not directly our work as missionaries. The establishment and building up of the Church is our work . . .

The Church progresses as a conquering power, not as one who goes about merely to capture individual souls. The salvation of souls is a very definite kind of work: it is salvation through the Church; let the Church be established and souls will be saved.[12]

This specific formulation of the missionary aim of the Church is more than merely the opinion of some theologians. It has become the official guiding principle of Catholic missionary activity, clearly and repeatedly announced by the successors of St. Peter. As this point seems to have been overlooked by a number of modern mission-theorists, it might be well to cite here some of the more pertinent papal statements:

What is the object of these holy missions, we ask, except that the Church of Christ be instituted and established in so vast a number of places? And how shall the Church be built up today among the nations. . . ?[13]

---

[12] *The Collected Works of Abbot Vonier*, vol. 2, Newman, Westminster, 1952, pp. 123–124.

[13] Pius XI: "*Quorsum, quaesumus, sacrae missiones pertinent, nisi ut in tanta immensitate locorum Ecclesia Christi instituatur ac stabiliatur? Et unde haec apud ethnicos hodie constabit. . . . ?*" Rerum Ecclesiae, *AAS*, 1926, p. 74.

Whenever the local clergy exist in sufficient numbers, and are suitably trained and worthy of their holy vocation, there you may rightly say that the work of the missionaries has been successfully completed and the Church has been well founded.[14]

As everyone knows, the primary concern of these holy missions is that the light of Christian truth should be fully manifested to new peoples so that new Christians may be formed. To attain, however, this ultimate objective it is necessary—and this must always be kept in sight—that the Church be firmly established among other peoples and placed under its own indigenous hierarchy.[15]

The primary object of missionary endeavor, namely, the foundation of the Church of God among native peoples . . .[16]

The proper end of missions is to plant the Church in new lands in such a way that after having become deeply rooted, they can prosper and grow without the help of foreign missionaries.[17]

Missionary activity is primarily a matter of spreading out to more and more *new peoples,* rather than concentrating on the conversion of every single person in one particular place, especially when an indigenous Church has already been raised up once among the people of that particular place. This kind of

[14] Benedict XV: *"Ubicumque igitur quantum sat est indigenae cleri eiusque bene instituti et vocatione sua sancta digni, ibi missionarii opus feliciter expletum Ecclesiamque præclare esse fundatum iure dixeris."* Maximum Illud, AAS, 1919, p. 445.

[15] Pius XII: *"Eo autem, ut omnes norunt, hae sacrae expeditiones primo loco spectant, ut christianae veritatis lumen novis gentibus luculentius effulgeat, utque novi habeantur christiani. Ad illud tamen, extremam veluti metam, contendant necesse est, quod quidem semper ante mentis oculos esse debet, ut nempe Ecclesia apud alios populos firmiter constabiliatur eidem propria, ex indigenis delecta, tribuatur Hierarchia."* Evangelii Praecones, AAS, 1951, p. 507.

[16] Pius XII, *Epist.,* November 11th, 1954, *AAS,* 1954, p. 703.

[17] Pius XII, at the opening of St. Peter's College in Rome; quoted in *The Church. A Divine Mystery,* by Roger Hasseveldt, Fides, Notre Dame, 1954, p. 173.

concentration leads to the stagnation of missionary activity, the "choke-law," as we have seen in Chapter 1; and so it leads to the death of the indigenous Church, which turns its missionary zeal inward on its own people, to the neglect of those others for whom the sign of salvation has not yet been manifested. The faith and the love of a person or of a people must inevitably die, if they are not primarily turned outward to others. Our faith and our love are fulfilled and enriched only to the extent of our giving them to others. This giving is the source of our own vitality and the cause of our hope. Everything must die, one way or another. But as the Gospel teaches, by dying to ourselves for the sake of others, we live. Christ's total donation of Himself gave life to the world. And so it must be with each person and every community of persons who accept the chalice of faith and of love. It is not easy to be a Christian. But it is now the only hope of life.

We know from the lessons of Church history that much mischief has already been done through efforts to convert (one way or another) to visible membership in the Church every single person in one place or another. At one time, this was held as a goal of the Church in the "Christian" states of Europe. But now such a goal appears to have been motivated more by political expediency than by sound theology. "It was," in the words of Karl Rahner, "a fact of cultural history rather than of theology."[18] This achievement was largely quantitative, with the durability of an earthly kingdom resting on foundations of sand. Is it possible that the present "defection of the masses" in some of these same regions may be essentially a kind of "natural" consequence of Christendom's questionable "supernatural" achieve-

---

[18] *The Christian Commitment,* by Karl Rahner, S.J., Sheed & Ward, New York, 1964, p. 31.

ment? "Of all that was done in the past, we eat the fruit, either rotten or ripe."[19] For historical and sociological reasons, as we have remarked, Christianity was once looked on as a religion of numerically quantitative growth, eventually and inevitably destined to embrace visibly every single person on earth. But it is now recognized as a religion of free choice and deliberate commitment. The dream of total populations becoming simultaneously and homogeneously Christian is now past. If we try to pursue this medieval ideal in the context of the modern world, we are going to distort completely the meaning of the Church's missionary and eschatological goals. The measure of the Church's achievement in the world, if it can be measured, is not in terms of the number of individual believers here or there or now or then. Let it be considered only in terms of the peoples for whom the sign of their salvation has not yet been raised up once in the sacramentally symbolic *Lumen Gentium* established among them on—it is necessary to insist again—firm and indigenous foundations. This is the goal of missionary activity. And it can be attained.

3. St. Paul

Such is the orientation of missionary activity reflected in the Acts of the Apostles, and especially in the life of St. Paul:

... what Christ had wrought in me to bring about the obedience of the nations ... so that from Jerusalem round about as far as Illyricum I have *completed* the evangelization of Christ.

But I have not preached the Gospel where Christ has already been named, lest I might build on another man's foundation; but even as

[19] T. S. Eliot.

it is written, "They who have not been told of him shall see, and they who have not heard shall understand."[20]

How often did St. Paul leave his former mission-stations where his "work had been *finished*," after he had "opened to the peoples the door of faith?"[21] He returned to his Christian communities only for passing visits while on his way to new peoples.[22] While we know from his letters that all was not always well with the young churches, and certainly not every individual in these places had been converted, St. Paul was nevertheless constrained to continue moving on to more and more new peoples who had not yet been evangelized, so that through him "the preaching of the Gospel might be *completed,* and that all the nations might hear."[23] There is a time for each people, as for the whole world, when missionary activity is "finished" and "completed."

St. Paul's concept of missionary activity was one of founding the Church among all peoples in as short a time as possible; for he was consumed with the desire of the Lord's return, which could happen only after the completion of this mission of making Christ sacramentally present to every nation. ". . . and tell us what will be the sign of Your coming and of the end of the world?"[24]

The Gospel must *first* be preached all over the world, for a sign to all nations . . . and *then* shall the end come.[25]

The hope and expectation of the first Christians was not as lethargic as ours today. They were not even very patient, wish-

---

[20] Rom 15:19–21.
[22] Rom 15:22–29.
[24] Mt 24:3.

[21] Acts 14:25–27.
[23] 2 Tim 4:17.
[25] Mk 13:10; Mt 24:14.

ing even to hasten, if possible, the coming of the Lord, knowing all the while that "the Lord is not being dilatory over his promise . . . only giving more time, because his will is that all . . . should attain repentance, not that some should be lost."[26] Even the young churches sent out missionaries to the non-evangelized peoples,[27] for they were hastening toward the day of the Lord.[28] The Christians of Antioch made full use of the grace given "to announce among the nations good tidings."[29] It was a matter of laying the foundations of the Church among more and more new peoples:

According to the grace of God which has been given to me, as a wise builder, I laid the foundation, and another builds thereon.[30]

The missionary lays the foundation and then moves on,[31] while the indigenous pastor builds thereon: "if his work abides which he has built thereon . . . *if* his work burns . . ."[32]

4. *Implications*

The Christians of Antioch did not all remain in that city in order to convert everyone there before sending missionaries elsewhere. This missionary aim of spreading out among more and more new peoples, rather than concentrating on one or another particular people, is also expressed in the Church's practical directives to missionaries in the field. We have seen an example of this in reference to the "choke-law." Pius XI, writing to those in charge of mission jurisdictions, put it thus:

[26] 2 Pt 3:9.   [27] Acts 13:1-4.
[28] 2 Pt 3:11-12.   [29] Eph 3:8.
[30] 1 Cor 3:10.   [31] 1 Cor 1:17.
[32] 1 Cor 3:14-15.

See to it that the missionaries are so distributed that no part of your territory is neglected and that no part is left for future evangelization.[33]

And Pius XI instructed that, once the goal has been attained of establishing the Church firmly under its own native hierarchy, missionaries should gladly move on to begin again somewhere else; for "sowers and cultivators of the divine word do not take up permanent abode in apostolic fields already harvested."[34] The missionary societies "possess no permanent title to their mission areas."[35] Thus, when the Church has been "securely established" among a people, "then it is time for superiors to send their men on, . . . leaving the harvest to be reaped by others."[36] And in an instruction of the Sacred Congregation de Propaganda Fide:

If care is not taken in good time to train the local clergy, then it will soon happen that the missionary, whose aim is the preaching of the Gospel to pagans, will limit himself to a Christian community and will abandon unbelievers almost completely.[37]

This instruction goes on to say that, with the establishment of the local clergy, the missionaries will be freed for their proper

[33] *"Itaque cum catholici inter ethnicos apostolatus magnam partem in vos recidat exitus, res aptius volumus a vobis ordinari, ut facilior posthac ad christianae sapientiae propagationem pateat aditus et numerus eorum augeatur quibus ea feliciter collucet. Sacros igitur praecones ita vobis cordi sit dispertire, ut nulla territorii pars ab evangelii praedicatione vacet et in aliud tempus excolenda reservetur. Quare longius, per mansiones, procedite, missionalibus in aliquo loco, quasi quodam centro, constituendis, quem locum minores undique stationes circumstent, uni saltem catechistae commissae et sacra aedicula auctae, quasi missionales e sede media identidem, stato scilicet tempore, ministerii causa, adeant atque invisant."* Rerum Ecclesiae, Typis Polyglottis Vaticanis, Rome, 1926, p. 20.

[34] *Evangelii Praecones, op. cit.,* p. 46, nos. 34–35.

[35] *Rerum Ecclesiae,* by Pius XI, *loc. cit.,* p. 22.

[36] *Maximum Illud,* by Benedict XV, tr. by W. Connolly, in *Catholic Missions,* p. 21, no. 35.

[37] *AAS,* 1923, pp. 370–371.

work among other non-evangelized peoples, instead of being absorbed in the pastoral care of the gradually increasing Christian community among one particular people.

Implied in all of this are further considerations of a human and psychological nature. Abraham was the first Christian missionary:

By faith . . . he obeyed by going out into a place which he was to receive for an inheritance; and he went out not knowing where he was going. By faith, he abode in the land of promise as in a foreign land, dwelling in tents with Isaac and Jacob . . . for he was looking for a city with fixed foundations, of which city the architect and the builder is God.[38]

If all missionaries lived in tents, as did Abraham, it might be much easier for them to uproot themselves and move on to new lands of promise when once the fixed foundations have been firmly laid by God through their efforts among one people. Yet some missionaries have a tendency to fix their own foundations and to remain forever "where Christ has already been named." This causes human tensions between themselves and the local clergy—who are happy to have the missionaries remain as helpers in building up the young churches, but who are also understandably relieved when the missionaries finally depart for new lands.

We have an example of this very problem today in certain dioceses of North America. Foreign clergy had to be recruited in earlier times for the pastoral care of the faithful who were originally immigrant Catholics. These pastors from overseas helped to preserve the faith, which eventually flourished and gave rise to a local clergy. Much to the dismay of the new native clergy, however, "the others"—inevitably retaining the

38 Heb 11:8–10.

thought-patterns of their own original culture regardless of how long they had been among "the natives"—continued to control the Church's pastoral functions. The solution, at least as far as missionaries would be concerned in a similar situation, is quite simple: Move on. The actual time of departure would, of course, be determined by the mutual agreement of the responsible authorities after consultation with members of both the missionary and the pastoral clergy working in the area. Naturally, the decision must be executed over a period of some length for the good of all concerned. For this human tension is in itself an important and healthy sign, manifesting at once the vigor of the young Church and the termination of missionary activity. Missionary activity among a people belongs to a limited period with both a beginning and an end. The missionary himself hastens toward the end of this period among one people after another; and he hastens all men toward the end of all time. Like time itself, he moves toward, and signifies visibly, his own termination.

All of this shows that missionary activity comes to an end among a particular people well before every single individual in that one place has been converted to visible membership in the Church, if indeed this sort of total conversion ever takes place anywhere. Furthermore, if this were to happen everywhere, Christians could no longer be witnesses, for the very notion of witness is redundant where the truth is already known to all. In any case, the Church, once firmly established through a sufficiently significant nucleus of the people, is itself capable of internal growth, calling into the visible fold more and more of God's chosen witnesses from among this particular people, even as the young churches of apostolic times, after the work of the first missionaries had been completed among their people, "grew stronger and stronger in the faith and increased in numbers daily."[39] For the Church is "the sign raised up among the nations, inviting all who have not yet believed."[40] It is the leaven of hope among the people. It is the salt of the earth. It is the fig tree which is meant to bear fruit.

While the missionaries from abroad are primarily and directly concerned with the less personal work of establishing the Church through a core of believers among the people taken in their totality, the local pastoral clergy are primarily and directly concerned with the care and the increase of the flock in its gradual extension to more and more persons among their own people. With the completion of missionary activity under the general direction of a foreign clergy, a more intensive pastoral activity comes into its own in the more relevant and personal medium of the indigenous culture and under the more intimate guidance of the local clergy. In the words of Pope Pius XII:

There are many countries that have long since outstripped the missionary stage of their ecclesiastical organization and are governed by their own hierarchy, contributing to the whole Church both the material and spiritual benefits of which, formerly, they were only the recipients.[41]

The young churches are at the same time the one, catholic, and apostolic Church. And, as we have seen, the *raison d'être* and goal of all is the same: to become in historical tangibility among all peoples the sacramental *Lumen Gentium:*

For indeed, the Church was born precisely for this, to spread the Kingdom of Christ throughout the whole world. . . .[42]

---

[39] Acts 16:5.   [40] Vatican Council I, *DB*, no. 1794.

[41] Christmas Message, 1945, *AAS*, 1946, p. 18.

[42] Pius XI: *"Neque enim ad aliud nata Ecclesia est, nisi ut, regno Christi ubique terrarum dilatando . . ." Rerum Ecclesiae, loc. cit.*, p. 5.

The objective, therefore, is not "merely to guard the Lord's flock from danger," but *especially* to make every effort to gather the flock among others.[43] It is not enough that the young churches should be capable of caring for their own needs and running their local affairs. The measure of the Church's maturity anywhere is her missionary commitment to the remaining non-evangelized peoples of the world. So, if the young churches are to grow into their full maturity, and indeed to maintain the faith they have received, it is imperative that they should move progressively outward with the true spirit of Christian hope and love to those other peoples who have not yet known Christ. For the whole Church in each of her local manifestations is true to the inner demands of her life only to the extent that she increasingly signifies, through her historical work of becoming the *Lumen Gentium,* Christ and what He has done "once for all" to men everywhere. Wherever, therefore, the Church is exclusively absorbed in the care of herself—whether in a mission area, a parish, a diocese, a region, a nation, or a religious community —there she signifies nothing but her own death. "The Church's unique mission," in the words of Father de Lubac, "is that of making Christ present to men. She is to announce Him, show Him, and give Him, to all; the rest is superabundance."[44] Thus, it is that all true pastoral activity within the local churches generates new missionary activity, and missionaries continue to go out to other peoples in response to the Lord's call which

[43] *Ibid.:* ". . . *quisquis autem est, qui Iesu Pastorum Principis vices in terris divinitus gerat, is tantum abest ut dumtaxat in tuendo ac servando, quem regundum accepit, grege dominico possit acquiescere, ut contra, praecipuo muneri suo desit, nisi alienos externosque Christo lucrari atque adiungere omni contentione nitatur.*"

[44] *The Splendor of the Church,* by Henri de Lubac, S.J., Sheed & Ward, New York, 1956, p. 161.

resounds from age to age: "Leave your country, your kinfolk, and your father's house, for the land which I will show you."[45]

It is well known that today certain lands are closed to Christian missionaries from Europe and America. The reasons for closing the doors are not always and only religious. Some of these areas may still remain opened to missionaries from neighboring countries of similar ethnic-culture backgrounds. This challenge faces the young churches today in certain parts of the world; and it may well be the test of their faith. Are they ready and willing to step into the breach by making all of the catholic sacrifices demanded of this new situation? The missionary calling from the Lord of the harvest is not directed merely to European and American Christians, but to all who believe that He is the Messiah, the Son of God, for whose coming the whole world has been waiting.[46]

It is a fact that some of the young churches have been more abundantly blessed with priestly and religious vocations than some of the older dioceses, which nevertheless continue to send missionaries abroad. The making of generous sacrifices for the missions is therefore presented to them, not as a mere possibility, but as an urgent demand. The faith which is not communicated to others will be lost. For "the catholic vitality of the Church in a nation is measured by the sacrifices it is capable of making for the missionary cause . . ."

The missionary spirit and the catholic spirit are one and the same thing. This is true to such an extent that a Christian is not truly faithful and devoted to the Church if he is not *equally* attached and devoted to her universality, desiring that she take root and flourish in all parts of the world.[47]

[45] Gen 12:1.   [46] Jn 11:27.
[47] *Fidei Donum,* by Pius XII, *AAS,* 1957, p. 370.

Growth in holiness [among Christians] will be in proportion to their active interest in the holy missions.[48]

Have missionaries from Europe and America built well in Asia and Africa and Oceania? We shall see very soon. The time of testing is upon us. By their fruits they shall be known. If the leaven should fail to raise up the flour . . . If the salt loses its savor . . . If the fig tree bears no fruit . . . Such is the life of the Church in time. The process is eschatological. The opportunity is "once for all." The present moment of decision and of action in the historical human condition does not recur.

The whole Church is catholic and missionary from her very origin to her final destiny, from the resurrection to the Parousia. But it is only through the gradual movement of history that she is able to become in actuality, and in the sight of all men, what she is in her nature and in her aspirations. To do this she must have a reasoned plan for, and an organized approach to, the evangelization of the world. The basic principles of catholic missionary activity are contained in the officially formulated directives and in the practice of the Church. It is for us to search the fuller meaning of these principles, and to make the applications within our own historical time and place. Life is short, and we are compelled by the circumstances of our historical existence to make decisions today and lay our plans of action for tomorrow. We must do this in the light of what little understanding we have. We cannot wait for professional scholars to answer all of our questions. For, when all is said and done, we are going to be judged very soon on our here-and-now commitments without which the best of theories are quite irrelevant. Yet it is possible for us to go a little further beyond the Church's official formulations of our guiding principles. By considering the missionary

[48] *Evangelii Praecones*, by Pius XII, *AAS*, 1951, p. 507.

significance of salvation, the nations, and the Church, we may be in a better position to see why our missionary aims are what they are.

There is no real progress without some bringing up of matters afresh or some change of perspective, some break or some turning back, a resumption of contact with the ground of the original data.[49]

[49] *Further Paradoxes,* by Henri de Lubac, S.J., Newman, Westminster, 1958, p. 5.

III.

Salvation

He recapitulates in Himself the long history of men, summing up
and giving us salvation . . .

St. Irenaeus

The meaning of salvation is no mere academic question for the
missionary. It is the practical question of the day, every day.
Aware of the immense number of people whom he knows but
cannot reach with his saving message, the missionary tends to
state the question in words very much like those of Dante:

A man is born on the shores of the River Indus, and there is no one
there to tell him of Christ . . . All his desires and deeds are good, so
far as human reason sees, sinless in life or speech. He dies unbaptized
and without faith; where is that justice which condemns him?[1]

To the small company of conservative theologians who see the
salvation of the "heathen" only in terms of explicit faith in Christ,
and would therefore have missionaries concerned mainly with
"converting" to visible membership in the Church as many individuals as possible anywhere and everywhere, one might also
say with Dante: "Now who are you to sit in judgment from a
thousand miles away. . . ? To this kingdom never ascended
anyone who did not believe in Christ, either before or after He
was nailed to the cross. But see, many cry 'Christ! Christ!' who
at the Last Judgment shall be further away from Him than many

---

[1] *Paradiso,* canto XIX, vv. 70–78.

who knew Him not."[2] And to those who would place human and logical limits on the magnanimity of God, one might say with St. Cyprian:

The Spirit pours Himself out generously: no levee can block His path, no restraining wall hinder His expansion. He wells forth unceasingly; He overflows, inundates all . . .[3]

The poetry is true and the rhetoric sound. But why? It is necessary to go a little deeper. We want to know just how possible and how available salvation really is for the vast majority of mankind who, through no fault of their own, have not and will not hear explicitly the Gospel message. We want also to know precisely in what this salvation consists, and how it is made available to all men.

1. The Same Possibility for All

The unique Christ-event, saving the whole of mankind, took place once within the framework of man's long historical pilgrimage on earth. This was a concrete event of history, occurring at a precise time and a specific place among a particular people. Generations of biological and historical preparation, guided by the hand of God, had preceded this actual advent on earth of the Messiah sent by God for the sole purpose of saving all peoples.[4] This was the historical mission of the Son of Man Who is one with the Father who sent Him.[5] This was the physical presence in created flesh of the archetype and cause of all creation, saving

[2] Ibid., vv. 79–81, 103–108.
[3] Epistolae, 1:5, PL 4, 203; quoted by Emile Mersch, S.J., The Whole Christ, Bruce, Milwaukee, 1938, p. 233.
[4] Lk 2:30–31; 1 Tim 1:15.   [5] Jn 7:16; 14:9–11.

all from within.[6] And "by reason of this body," wrote St. Hilary, "all humanity is contained in Him . . .":[7]

Being made of the Virgin, He took in Himself the "reality" of the flesh. Thus, the whole human race is united in Him and sanctified in Him. And, as all are restored in Him through the body which He willed to take, so too does He take up His abode spiritually in all.[8]

So the historical Savior, who lived among some men for the enlightenment of all and Who died at the hands of some men because of the sins of all, was "in the world but not of the world."[9] His saving action was in time, but not of time. For it was the historical manifestation of an eternal act of God's saving and all-embracing love, accomplished by the God-Man within the exigencies of the human condition, and valid for all men of all times—for every man who comes into the world, whether before or after this signal event.

The Divine Word, through Whom all things are made, is the same re-making power of Christ, enlightening every man who comes into the world; "and of His fullness we have all received, grace for grace."[10] According to St. Irenaeus, "The Word was ever present to the human race, until the day when He united Himself with His creature, and was made flesh."[11] What He has done historically "once for all"[12] through the Incarnation, He has done from the beginning of time, giving grace for grace to each previous period in the unfolding history of mankind's salvation. This also He does for all subsequent generations of men who are

---

[6] Col 1:15–20; Heb 2:10; 5:1–3.
[7] *Comment. in Mt.,* 4:12, *PL* 935; quoted by Mersch, *op. cit.,* p. 293.
[8] *De Trinitate,* 2:25, *PL* 66; *ibid.,* p. 297.
[9] Jn 1:10; 17:15.   [10] Jn 1:1–18.
[11] *A.H.,* III, 16, 6, *PG* 925; quoted by Mersch, *op. cit.,* p. 233.
[12] Heb 7:27–28; 9:26–27.

not yet within time. "It is done! I am the Alpha and the Omega . . . To him who thirsts I will give of the fountains of the water of life freely. He who overcomes shall possess these things, and I will be his God, and he shall be My son."[13]

From the beginning to the end of time, each period in this history (including every concrete ethnic-culture situation in which men individually experience some fraction of this total history) is an integral part of mankind's salvation. The whole eschatological process is at once universal and particular, eternally actual and historically concrete, with a beginning and an end; each of its preceding and subsequent events is significant only in relation to the whole: what went before is no less valid than what follows, just as what follows derives meaning from, and manifests the meaning of, what went before. God does not forget that the salvation obtained by Christ is for all men in whatever temporal and historical conditions they may find themselves; for it is He who puts them where they are.

It would be quite wrong to imagine in this connection that what has happened at "the fullness of time" in "the latter days" of the world (or in the later historical ages of different peoples) has no intrinsic bearing on the human events of all previous times, as well as of present and subsequent times. St. Leo the Great reminds us, in his third sermon for Christmas, that "the Incarnation of the Word produced its effects not only after, but also before its realization in time, and the mystery of man's salvation was never, in any age of antiquity, at a standstill. . . . From the foundations of the world He ordained one and the same cause of salvation for all. For the grace of God, whereby the whole body of the saints is ever justified, was augmented by the birth of Christ; but it did not begin then."

[13] Ap 21:6–7.

So it is that the same Incarnate Word, the redeeming Christ of history, continues to save until the end with the same grace by which He has saved from the beginning. He who cries to God "from the ends of the earth"[14] is none other than the same saving Word, present everywhere to all men in every time; for, in the words of St. Augustine, "how can this one man cry out from the ends of the earth, unless He be one in all?"[15] Such is "the dispensation of the mystery which has been hidden from eternity in God, Who created all things; . . . according to the eternal purpose which He accomplished in Christ Jesus our Lord."[16]

God gives His Holy Spirit to all who obey Him:[17] to each man in the historical moments which are his own free experience of being on earth. Every man has his "hour of grace and trial," as Father Bernard Häring has put it so well: "Amid the forces that lie between the beginning and the end of time, he decides his destiny at each temporal moment in the light of the great ages of salvation."[18] He realizes his personal destiny in goodness or in evil, through a process of growth in one direction or another, within the historical context of the particular space and time given to him providentially for this very purpose.

History, as a genuine category of reality, relates past and present, but always with reference to the future in which all will be finally concluded through the transcendent Lord of history. For it is in and through Him that the free acts of men transcend biological space-time to reach the eternal God Who allows each man to say to Him "yes" or "no." And each of these free decisions

[14] Ps 60:3.
[15] In Ps., 54, PL 36, 640; quoted by Mersch, op. cit., p. 423.
[16] Eph 3:9-11.   [17] Acts 5:32.
[18] The Law of Christ, vol. 1, Newman, Westminster, 1961, p. 87.

influences the entire history of salvation, accepting or rejecting the call, making or unmaking the Kingdom, hastening or delaying the coming, saving or not saving the whole of mankind: "In each soul, God loves and partly saves the whole world which that soul sums up in an incommunicable and particular way."[19] Each of these decisions hastens or delays the day of the Lord's return at the end of time; for both the beginning and the present have meaning only in relation to the end:

> Time present and time past
> Are both perhaps present in time future,
> And time future contained in time past.[20]

Each man's growth to maturity is caused only gradually under his own principle of life, which is the same and equally valid at every stage of his development from birth to death. Such is the slowly maturing process of saving history. Such is the essence of the human condition. Each member of mankind, in his allotted time and place, treads for a short distance, with irreversible steps, along the same one-way road and under the same guiding light and for the same purpose. Adapting Himself to this condition of His own designing, God offers His saving grace only in and through history, granting to each stage its due of mankind's salvation already achieved once for all. "The grace of God our Savior has appeared to all men . . ."[21] For He is "the Lord of all,"[22] "the Lord of history";[23] "Who is and Who was and Who is coming . . ."[24] So the one history of salvation continues to ma-

[19] Teilhard De Chardin, *The Divine Milieu,* Harper, New York, 1960, p. 32.

[20] T. S. Eliot, "The Four Quartets," *The Collected Poems & Plays of T. S. Eliot,* Harcourt, Brace, New York, 1952, p. 117.

[21] Tit 2:11.   [22] Acts 10:36.

[23] 1 Tim 1:17.   [24] Ap 1:7–8.

ture gradually through the same salutary life principle offered with equal validity to all men: first in the gestation period of the saving Word, Who "in the fullness of time" brought forth from creation itself the Incarnate cause of salvation, Who now in these "latter days" continues to save until the world is fully prepared for His final coming in glory, when "every eye shall see Him, and they also who pierced Him. And all the tribes of the earth shall wail over Him."[25]

God truly wills that "all men should be saved and come to the knowledge of truth."[26] He does not delay in His promises, but He is "long suffering, not wishing that any should perish, but that all should return to repentance."[27] So in His own ways of saving faith He reveals Himself as an option offered to every man who comes into the world, and with due respect to the particular time and historical context in which each man is providentially placed. For each man and every event has its proper meaning within the total history of salvation, just as the historical events of Christ's life and death and resurrection give meaning to the whole. There is no injustice with God whose salvation is for all, and therefore offered freely to all. As God is no respecter of persons in the dispensation of His salutary love, neither is He bound to any particular times and places. While this offer of salvation is purely gratuitous, it is nonetheless real and salutary; for the vague sort of non-saving graces of which theologians sometimes speak would simply make a fiction of God's clearly stated wish that all men should be saved. He, Who is in the beginning and in the end, renders to each man according to his works.[28] He, for Whom one day is a thousand years and a thousand years as one day,

[25] *Ibid.*
[27] 2 Pt 3:9.
[26] 1 Tim 2:4.
[28] Ap 22:13; Rom 2:6.

does not delay in His promises.[29] He, Who does not wish that any should perish, comes quietly (as a thief) to each man and to every people and to the whole world before the end.[30] And for each man to whom God reveals Himself, in whatever way of faith and in whatever stage of the human condition, the acceptable time is always now.[31]

The significance of this "now" in which each man has his real participation, his moments of grace, of trial, and of decision, is basic to any appreciation of salvation's universal and corporate relevance in the dimensions of history. We might reflect, therefore, on Father Häring's concise exposition of this notion:

... the historic present (in the language of Holy Scripture the *kairos,* the hour of grace and trial granted to us by God) reaches out into past and future. The entire past enters the present as destiny. The past has its heritage (biological, cultural, moral-religious). . . . This treasure inherited from the past is a summons or invitation, and a challenge as well, to the free will of man in the historic moment of the present. . . . We must accept the destiny by our own free decision and within the limits it imposes set our wills to the good. Freedom can exercise itself only on the materials of the past, on the "destiny" of the historic heritage. The free will must seize this destiny and within its limits render its own unique decision.

To make a decision in the *kairos,* however, means again to pass on the historical heritage of the past new-formed, as fruit of one's own freedom, to the future. Accordingly, in the Now of history man must mold anew his own past and that of his forebears and be responsible for it anew. In this very way he is responsible to the future. The heritage of the past always bears within it the decisions of the present, the Now. In the present the call to man is always concrete and particular. But the decision of the Now also anticipates the future and establishes a pattern for the decisions which will follow.[32]

[29] 2 Pt 3:8–9.   [30] *Ibid.,* v. 10.
[31] 2 Cor 6:2.   [32] *Op. cit.,* p. 87–88.

By looking into his own heart, each one of us may glimpse the meaning of these conscious moments of inner decision brought to us through external historical events and situations which, in their more dramatic manifestations, leave us with a brief awareness either of joy or of guilt. How often, for example, have we been presented, under the multitudinous disguises of different times and places, with the universal situation which confronted a priest, a Levite, and a Samaritan on the same road going down from Jerusalem to Jericho? Or how often have we been haunted by the memory of the Lord's words: "I was hungry, and you ..."?

Salvation takes place on this level and in the realm of the human and historically significant decisions of the hour "made by individuals and valid for all men for all time," to use Guardini's phrase. Revelation shows us the historical significance of some of these decisions. If Adam had not failed ... If Abraham had failed ... If the leaders of the Jews had not rejected ... If Christ had refused ... If the Church today ... If you and I ... Such is the history of mankind's salvation. It is a matter of making decisions within the concrete historical situation, decisions which accept or reject a call to action, involvement, commitment, or mission in the here and now of history. Thus, with his own conscience bearing him witness, the offer of saving grace is made to each person in the *kairos* which is in time, but not of time. For this is "the providential moment of decision given with the grace of God"; and "this test means more than the mere preservation of the order of creation and the full acceptance of the historical heritage. It also opens to man the opportunity for the encounter with God through the historic and trans-historic union with Christ."[33] It is in these moments of free decision that each man proves himself before God, or he perishes.

[33] *Ibid.*, p. 91.

Thus, we glimpse to some extent the mystery of God's love for all, expressed by Himself to Moses: "I will have mercy on whom I will have mercy. . . ."[34] "So then," we read in the Epistle to the Romans, "there is no question of him who wills nor of him who runs, but only of God showing mercy. For the Scripture says to Pharaoh, 'For this very purpose I have raised you up that I may show in you My power, and that My name may be proclaimed in all the earth.' Therefore, He has mercy on whom He will, and whom He will He hardens."[35] Yet the goodness of God and the witness of each man's conscience in the *kairos* are meant to lead men to repentance.[36] To some this is justice and to others judgment. But by the saving grace of God, eternal life is truly given to those who "by patience in good works seek glory and honor and immortality."[37] even though these works themselves are possible only in virtue of this same saving grace.[38] As "the grace of God our Savior has appeared to all men,"[39] so *the real possibility of accepting this grace is the same for all,* whenever and wherever they may live on earth. From this historical viewpoint of salvation, therefore, men today are no worse off than those who lived in the actual historical presence of Christ; nor were the Jews any better off than the Gentiles:

For there is no distinction, as all have sinned and have need of the glory of God. They are justified freely by his grace through the redemption. . . . For there is but one God Who will justify . . . through the same faith.[40]

[34] Rom 9:15. [35] Rom 9:16–18.
[36] Rom 2:4,15. [37] Rom 2:7.
[38] Phil 2:13; Eph 2:8–10. [39] Tit 2:11.
[40] Rom 3:23–31; "Under different signs there is the same faith," wrote St. Augustine concerning "all those who believed at the time of Abraham, Isaac, Jacob, etc." *Tractatus in Jn. Evang.,* 45, 9; *PL* 35, 1722–23; quoted by Abbé R. Hasseveldt, *The Church. A Divine Mystery,* p. 8.

In their rational approaches to this mystery of salvation, theologians have divided grace into a large number of categories. But despite all of these subtle distinctions, which are not without value, saving grace is one: from the same cause (God's love), through the same source (the Incarnate Word), and for the same purpose (mankind's salvation). The saving grace offered to Abel is the very same as that which is offered to men today and tomorrow. The same possibility for salvation exists for all men in the freedom of the historical *kairos* which is a real experience for all. "Two cities, the one of the wicked and the other of the saints, cover the whole period from the beginnings of the human race until the end of time."[41] By the free gift of saving grace, Abel was justified,[42] and he is venerated today as a saint in the Christian liturgy. Countless others, known and unknown, have also come to God through the saving belief "that God exists and is a rewarder to those who seek Him."[43] For by faith "the men of old had testimony borne to them . . ."[44] "In the way of faith all these died without receiving the promises, but beholding them afar off and acknowledging that they were pilgrims and strangers on earth. . . ; they seek after a better, that is, a heavenly country. Therefore, God is not ashamed to be called their God, for He has prepared for them a city."[45] By this same grace, Cornelius, who was neither a Jew nor a Christian, was "devout and God-fearing."[46] Accordingly, in this context, we may make

[41] St. Augustine, *De Catech. Rud.*, 3; quoted by J. Daniélou, *Holy Pagans of the Old Testament*, Helicon, Baltimore, 1957, p. 10.

[42] Mt 23:35; 1 Jn 3:12; Heb 11:4, 12:24.

[43] Heb 11:6; these words refer to Henoch, who in the Bible represents "man" (the meaning of the name); cf. Daniélou, *op. cit.*, p. 42ff.

[44] Heb 11:2.   [45] Heb 11:13–16.

[46] Acts 10:2.

our own these words of St. Peter, witnessing to the inner action of grace among pagans:

Now I really understand that . . . in every nation he who fears Him and does what is right is acceptable to Him . . . through Jesus Christ (who is the Lord of all). . . . Therefore, if God gave to them the same grace as He gave to us who believed in the Lord Jesus Christ, who was I that I should be able to interfere with God? . . . To the nations also God has given repentance unto life.[47]

What was possible for Abel is, for the very same reasons, possible for all men: a personal communication with God in faith and love and hope, as a foretaste and a pledge of each man's fulfillment in God. As with Abel, so with all men, this saving communion is available by the mercy of God Who alone initiates and accomplishes this new orientation of life, away from the congenital sinfulness and fundamental egotism of the human condition, toward the loving freedom of the sons of God; while man's highest contribution to this essential option of grace is nothing more than a natural and ineffectual desire for the fulfillment of his destiny in relation to God, with the concomitant attempts to live accordingly. The good works of men in their daily lives, through which this fundamental option and new orientation in grace becomes incarnate and mature, are salutary only by the grace of God offered in the *kairos*.

While these human acts are experientially isolated in their historical aspect of transitoriness, they have their lasting significance in the total orientation of a man's life in relation to his neighbor and to his God. Love is not a matter of this or that act merely; it is an orientation of one's life. So God does not give little graces here and there merely for isolated actions, or just to test man's responses in the way that a scientist might shoot

[47] Acts 10:34-36; 11:17-18.

charges of electricity into mice in order to study their reactions before increasing the charge. All grace is one, and given for the purpose of saving the entire life of the whole man, and of all mankind.[48]

This same saving grace is, therefore, available to all men everywhere, as an equally valid possibility in any and every historical context. Thus the meaning which St. Paul gave to these words of Isaiah:

I was found by those who did not seek me; I appeared openly to those who made no inquiry of me.[49]

2. Encounter and Dialogue

The door of saving faith has already been opened once for all men by the work of the Incarnate Word in time, but not of time. As there is no before or after with God's love, it remains for each individual man in his own existential condition to accept God's invitation by stepping through this door under the free impulse of grace offered in the *kairos:* the acceptable time which is always the "now," the moments of each man's deliberate moral decisions made in the context of his own historical experience, and guided by his own conscience. For each of these free acts places man "in the dialogue with the eternal God,"[50] before Whom he responds with his personal "yes" or "no," accepting or rejecting God's call. By the mercy of God some men take this step, and others do not; some obey the will of God, and others do not. God

[48] Karl Rahner has noted that "St. Thomas considered the actual acts of 'preparation' as acts of justification 'taking over,' done with the grace of justification already present . . ." *Nature and Grace,* Sheed & Ward, New York, 1963, p. 16.

[49] Rom 10:20; Is 65:1; *Denz.,* 176.   [50] Häring, *op. cit.,* p. 89.

knows His own and they know Him, wherever and whenever He may find them wandering on this earth: "Those whom He has foreknown He has predestined,"[51] and they accept His invitation to personal communion in the love of friendship, between Creator and creature, made possible by the Incarnation and made real by a "new inner vitality" created in the hearts of men beloved of God. By this created bond of grace, then, man is able to reciprocate with the same love with which he was first loved by God, with the constancy of this new friendship depending only on Him Who initiates the dialogue and brings it to fruition in final salvation. As Father David Burrell has said:

Our union with God in this life is not yet sheer fruition, but rather one of detachment and growth, comprehending profound consent and gnawing concern in a synthesis that spells life, motion, pilgrimage. God is in us working our salvation so that we too may accomplish it, by faith and hope that issue in love. . . . It is His presence to the soul (or better, the soul's presence to Him) that works the dialogue of living faith through the "second nature" of created grace with its consequent habits and gifts.[52]

This salvation, although essentially dependent on the redeeming Christ of history, is nevertheless truly universal and comprehends the whole history of redeemed mankind. For the Incarnate Word Who appeared once in history is the same Word of God Who is present to all of His creatures from the beginning to the end, saving men from within themselves, by revealing Himself personally in the experiential dialogue which needs no human words conceptually formulated. This one creating and re-creating Word in each man's inner being is enough. The saving grace of friendship between Creator and creature is, in the words of

[51] Rom 8:29.
[52] "Indwelling: Presence and Dialogue" by D. Burrell, C.S.C., *Theological Studies,* March 1961, vol. 22, no. 1, p. 12.

Burrell, "the immediate consciousness of an affinity, already mutual but hitherto unrevealed."[53] This friendship is, to be sure, precarious, for man himself is ever faithless and unworthy. Thus, all of the initiative comes from the faithful partner in this loving dialogue. The mutuality originates in God, for the presence of men to God precedes and transcends any experience men may have of God's presence within them. But He is present in the souls of the just, and personally so, even before His created grace manifests His presence in the vague and unformulated experiential response of man's faith and hope and love. So in a very real sense it is not primarily created grace which constitutes salvation for men, but the living presence of God in those whom He deigns to justify by means of created grace as the instrument whereby creatures may respond to His presence in a communion of love. It is a personal communion, for "no action of God can be impersonal."[54]

God Himself gives witness of His saving love for all men. His testimony is in the eternal Word made manifest in Scripture, in Christ, and in the hearts of men. "Everyone who loves is born of God, and knows God, for God is love . . . and he who abides in love abides in God, and God in him."[55] This ability to abide in love is created grace by which the just man verifies and responds to the presence within himself of uncreated love. Man, from within the confines of biological space-time, is open to eternity through the *kairos;* and he is able to accept and endure God's

[53] *Ibid.,* p. 5

[54] *Ibid.,* p. 11. "We are closer, more transparent, finally more supple to Him than we are to ourselves—be it as creatures or as adopted sons. . . . Since it is this personal presence to God which, willed, gives us existence, there is no opposition in God between presence and actuation. Causality is not an impersonal category when God is causing. The personal element . . . is always there" (p. 7).

[55] 1 Jn 4:7–8, 16.

offer of friendship only through God's adapting Himself to creation through created grace, given to man as he is in his own historical context in terms of which he makes his personal response. When a missionary arrives at a certain point in the history of a people who have not yet known Christ, he must understand, therefore, that saving grace has preceded him. As Father Rahner tells us:

> The grace of God has always been there ahead of our preaching; a man is always in a true sense a Christian already when we begin to commend Christianity to him. For he is a man already included in God's general will for salvation, redeemed by Christ, with grace already living and working in his innermost heart at least as the proffered possibility of supernatural action. . . . Any communication of Christianity is always a communication of what is already there, alive, within a man. . . .
>
> Life, as such, in the concrete, everyday life, has an inward openness to God through that grace which is constantly being offered to it, grace which desires to become living and fruitful in the very concreteness of this life. Joy, seriousness, responsibility, daring, commitment to an unforeseeable future, love, birth, the burden of work, and thousands of other aspects of life which everyone experiences have an undercurrent which comes from grace and leads to it, if they are rightly interpreted and really accepted in their true, undiluted being. It is on this supposition that we can hope that there are many who are Christians without explicitly knowing it, that grace is more widely accepted than is recorded in the Church's statistics. . . .[56]

All of this is true because a man is saved, whether he be a visible member of the Church or not, essentially by the saving and eternal will of God Who initiates and completes this work through His interior grace created in the souls of those whom He saves with His universally salvific will; and because the concrete order in which all men live is that of redeemed mankind: a

[56] *The Christian Commitment*, pp. 156–158; see also *Nature and Grace*, p. 32.

supernatural order in which the claims of God's grace are inescapable, inundating all.

But the essence of salvation is the loving presence to God from all eternity of the just whose actual salvation is made personal and responsive only in terms of creatureliness: created space and time and grace. For each in his own particular historical and biological context, indeed the whole of creation itself, is "nothing else than the constitution of the context needed for the self-expression of God"[57] outside of Himself. What, therefore, eminently constitutes this saving communion is the presence to God from all eternity of those whom He has first loved. Thus, Father Burrell's enlightening approach to this mystery, from the starting point of God's love for all men, is worth recording:

This personal grasp which God has of us is nothing less than our salvation. (And it would be the salvation of all men if it were not for sin, that terrible refusal to be human that admits of no explanation.) For our salvation is revealed and accomplished in Christ—not, to be sure, in such a way as to preclude coöperation . . . Rather, as eternity comprehends the unraveling of time in an ever-present now, so our salvation—the will and the achievement—is contained in the eternal act whereby the triune God redeemed us.[58]

Thus, the call to salvation comes from within man himself as he confronts the events of his daily existence. So the offer cannot be avoided by anyone. God wishes the salvation of all men, so each must freely decide for or against. Yet man's response to this offer of uncreated love is only through created grace. This response is a salutary act, although it is not final salvation; it is merely the beginning of a new life which may or may not be

[57] P. de Letter, S.J., "The Theology of God's Self-Gift," *Theological Studies,* September 1963, vol. 24, no. 3, p. 419.
[58] *Loc. cit.,* p. 7.

fulfilled.[59] For the final salvation of each man is worked out in fear and trembling,[60] only through the succession of free actions which constitute the total orientation of his whole life actually experienced in the context of his brief participation in the history of mankind. These salutary acts may, therefore, occur only once in the life of a man, or never, or frequently, depending only on the mercy of God's love. "The act itself of this encounter of God and man, which on earth can take place only in faith, is what we call salvation."[61] This is initiated by God's self-revelation in the souls of those whom He would save, and it is vitalized by His created grace, "the new inner vitality," by which man is able to respond to the divine advance. This is the only beginning and the only way of salvation for all who are saved, whether Christians, or Jews, or Pagans, or Mohammedans, or whatever.

This saving encounter is not an automatic consequence of merely external ritual actions. It is a real possibility for all men, even without the external helps and signs provided by organized religion. Even in the case of the Church's sacraments, which actually cause the grace which they signify, there is, in the words of Cardinal Gerlier, "no supernatural automatism, and sacramental action is not magic."[62] In each and every case, the fact of this encounter depends on God's prior gift of grace through which alone man is able to respond internally to what is externally offered in the sacraments, which are rendered ineffectual if the recipient is not already so disposed by God. As Archbishop Murray declared:

[59] Heb 6:4–12.   [60] Phil 2:12.

[61] *Christ the Sacrament of the Encounter with God,* by E. Schillebeeckx, O.P., Sheed & Ward, New York, 1963, p. 3.

[62] "The Co-existence of Believers and Unbelievers" by Cardinal Gerlier, *Cross Currents,* vol. 8, no. 3, p. 288.

No matter what the sacrament may be, no matter what the particular purpose or function to be discharged by that sacrament, it is always God that communicates Himself to us. . . . Unless one has been previously sanctified by the indwelling of the Holy Spirit, then the truth of God falls on deaf ears.[63]

Both Cain and Abel conformed their external actions to what was right, but only Abel was recognized by God as righteous.[64] So Father Schillebeeckx could say, in his treatment of the pre-sacramental bestowal of grace in "the desire" of those who have no explicit knowledge of Christ, that this is not "an extraordinary way of grace, but an initial stage . . . of the ordinary and universal mode of the bestowal of grace."[65] This beginning of the new life is the same for all men, and it is destined to grow to completion within the framework of history, in which only some men are chosen to participate visibly in the sacramental completion of the life of grace. In its historical completion, all grace is sacramental, but it is essentially the same and equally valid for all men in each stage of this historical movement of mankind's salvation.

"So from the justice of one man the result is unto the justification of life to all men."[66] As the representative of mankind, Christ accepted and made available the justice of God once for all. This is the salvation of the world: the mercy of God at the disposal of men. But this mercy justifies each man only in his own free, personal, and historical acceptance of his destiny in relation to God; and it transforms man into the likeness of Christ (even though he may have no historically explicit knowledge of Christ) Who in His death to Himself first accepted this justice for the sake of each man.

[63] "Homily" by J. G. Murray, S.T.D., *National Liturgical Week*, 1941, The Benedictine Liturgical Conference, Newark, 1942, p. 94.
[64] Daniélou, *op. cit.*, p. 30.   [65] *Op. cit.*, p. 179.
[66] Rom 5:18.

3. How Salvation Is Made Available

We have seen that "in every age of the world and in every generation the Lord has made purification and conversion possible to
all who sincerely turn to Him."[67] We have also considered the
essential meaning of salvation. Now it remains to be seen exactly
how it is possible for man freely to accept this gift of saving faith
without any explicitly formulated belief in Christ. How is salvation possible for the vast majority of mankind who have not
been historically called to visible membership in the Church?
Catholics have never held, at least officially, that no grace is bestowed on those outside the visible Church.[68] So what we are
offering here is not based on a novel concept, although this whole
matter has been considerably clarified by theologians since the
1949 condemnation by the Holy Office of Father Leonard
Feeney's extreme position.

Yet the practical attitude underlying that position still lingers
on to some extent. Some missionaries, having lost sight of the
goal of establishing the Church where she does not yet exist, are
obsessed with the aim of "converting" to visible membership in
the Church every single individual in one or another place, even
where these individuals may be believing Protestants. There is a
tacit assumption that salvation is really possible only for those
inside—as though these new "converts" did not still have to work
out their final salvation within their own family and social environments, amid the new human tensions sometimes resulting
from their individual conversions. Is the attainment of final salva-

---

[67] St. Clement of Rome, quoted by J. DeReeper, "The Problem of the
Salvation of the Heathen," *African Ecclesiastical Review,* July 1961, vol. 3,
no. 3, p. 166.
[68] *Denz.,* nos. 1379, 1295.

tion really easier and more assured for some than for others? Is not the condition of "fear and trembling" the same for all? Does not he to whom more is given incur the greater risk? It is well to give more attention to the approaches being made by contemporary theologians to this whole question of salvation outside the Church. The answers provided in the Middle Ages, and still repeated in our manuals of theology, are simply not enough, even when they are relevant.

The immensity of the question, with all of its practical implications, is only now being glimpsed, as we begin to see once again the dimensions of the missionary vision which drove St. Paul to the ends of his world. Our world is very much larger. And the theologians of the Middle Ages, on whom we have relied so heavily up to now, did not know this world of spherical geographical expanse and bursting populations. They did not know that the world is inhabited by more peoples not knowing Christ than knowing Him. They thought that the Gospel message, at least in its essential elements, had already reached most people in the world. The Crusades were to complete the evangelization process. So the few who bothered at all to treat the problem of salvation outside the visible Church did not even understand the question which is before our eyes today in all its drama. For them, a person who had not yet encountered the visible Church was an exception. So they talked about the *ordinary* way of salvation for most men (through visible membership in the Church), and the *extraordinary* way for the minority (by God explicitly sending someone to teach them, or Himself directly revealing what they must know in a special inspiration or illumination which produced explicit faith in Christ). This way of looking at the problem is still with us today. But if we take account of the facts, and if the words "ordinary" and "extraordinary" are to make any sense in the modern context of this question, then at least we should apply these terms differently, if not drop them altogether. Without raising this point of semantics, Father Schillebeeckx does actually transpose these words in his discussion of "extra-sacramental grace" which is the *ordinary* and initial and universal mode of the bestowal of grace for all men, and the only available way for most men.[69]

Father Max Seckler (writing in 1961) points out that St. Thomas in his early treatment of the question thought that all men had to have explicit faith in Christ in order to be saved, and so assumed the special intervention of God for the "extraordinary" cases of the minority of men who had not encountered the visible Church. But after the discovery of a few strange lands toward the end of his life, this notion of special intervention for the sake of explicit faith apparently was dropped. It does not appear in his *Summa Theologica,* where, although silent on this specific point, St. Thomas nevertheless does provide some very enlightening observations:

. . . For example, St. Thomas remarks that the good works of the yet-unbaptized Cornelius were pleasing to God because "he was not an infidel. . . . He had implicit faith, though the Gospel was not yet made known to Him" (*Summa Theol.,* II–II, q. 10, a. 4, ad 3).

According to St. Thomas (II *Sent.,* d. 28, q. 1, a. 1, ad 4), moral good and religious good are convertible. Both in faith as a saving act and in a clear moral decision, man asks and answers the question of life's meaning.

So for a man "to do what he can" is the same as "to answer the question about the meaning of life," or "to fulfill the laws of his nature." Thus, man's preparation for grace consists in doing what is good and true because it is good and true. This decision transcends the merely temporal utility of doing what is good and true and is

[69] *Op. cit.,* pp. 178–179.

therefore essentially religious (*in Boet. Trin.*, lect. 1, q. 1, a. 2, c). As a result, says St. Thomas, man's act becomes a saving act.

Such an act is saving simply because to do good for its own sake implies doing it in obedience to a law. Moral law, in turn points to a person who imposes it. In this way, man reaches some notion of God as a rewarder and so the possibility of faith. Grace is needed for this, but not a preacher or a private revelation.

Ultimately, faith expresses the dependence of the created soul on God, the First Truth. The same dependence is experienced in obeying an imposed law. The consciously made decision for the good and true transpires within the dimensions of life's destiny, salvation, and damnation. Man is drawn toward this decision by the urgent longing of the religiously significant inner instinct. And this man obediently surrenders his autonomous human behavior, owing to a concern for his salvation.

Such an obedient attitude justifies because it is one and the same God, the God of creation and salvation, Who is the object of faith and the goal of all desire. Whoever turns his life toward ultimate values, even though his ideas of God be vague, does not do so without grace.

A text of the *Summa Theologica* (I–II, q. 89, a. 6) shows how a saving act actually occurs in one who has not heard the Gospel. . . . As soon as a person reaches the age of reason, he necessarily asks what the meaning of life is. In answering the question he chooses for or against God, and in his choice decides his salvation: He is either justified or he sins mortally.

The act St. Thomas considers is the *first* moral act of a person, his first free response to the transcendental movement of God in him. It occurs in any kind of moral decision. For instance, whoever decides to tell the truth rather than to lie, not because otherwise he will be punished or for some similar motive, but because his conscience says he must be truthful, has performed his first moral act. In it he recognizes effectively an absolute law which stands over him; he has made contact with a value that is at once *his* good and *the* good. And to will the good because it is good is to will and love an ultimate value, *him who is good*.[70]

[70] Max Seckler, "Salvation for the Non-Evangelized," *Theology Digest,* Autumn 1961, vol. 9, no. 3, p. 168.

This line of argument is rather concise and subtle. But it is a way of showing how, without the aid of any external pedagogical and conceptual process, the non-evangelized may reach the real object of saving faith, through a knowledge which is vital and existential, but no less valid than the knowledge contained in the formulated ideas of the Gospel witness. For God did not leave Himself without testimony among the nations, bestowing blessings and filling the hearts of men with food and gladness.[71] All goodness and truth is only from God, so man's obedience to these values is achieved by God and leads back to Him Whose creative power makes, and Whose saving power re-makes with no less ease. So God, Who really acts in the conscience and the emotion and the reason of a person, makes Himself available as the experiential object of faith through the testimony of the religiously significant inner instinct of man's longing for what is good and true and saving. "This knowledge," says Father Seckler, "is neither explicit nor implicit in the usual meaning of these two terms, but it is a genuine knowledge resulting 'from a conformity to a morally good impulse.' This impulse is the voice of nature and is also the voice of God revealing Himself as the power of salvation."[72] Whoever submits his human autonomy to the good impulses of his conscience, obeys the voice of God; and whoever consistently resists self, dying daily to himself, through this obedience is walking with "a new inner vitality" along the one path which leads to final salvation.

Even those whose final salvation has come to completion through the historical testimony of the stone tablets of Israel and the formulated propositions of the Gospel witness in the sacramental Church, were nevertheless started on the way of salvation and brought to the end only through these very same salutary

[71] Acts 14:16.   [72] *Loc. cit.*

92

impulses acting within them and by the same saving power of God abiding in them. God's revealed plan of salvation is realized historically by means of the sacramental Church. But He does not save men with grace which He obtains from the sacraments of the Church. He makes His grace present in those whom He has first loved; and it is only because of this previous presence that the grace bestowed in the sacraments is efficacious in the completion of what has already begun. For the grace of the sacraments is the visible and historical completion of what is present already by the saving power of God disposing the recipient from within. It is only this internal saving action of God which gives fruitfulness to sacramental action in each of its visible enactments. As Father Schillebeeckx has noted, the "extra-sacramental" life of grace is the essential pre-condition, initiating what is brought to completion historically in the sacramental life of grace:

Within the totality of the risen Christ's eternal act of salvation, the bestowal of grace before the reception of the sacrament begins the historical realization of something that is brought to completion by the same eternal saving act, and that achieves the fullness of its historical manifestation in actual reception. . . . Depending as both do on God's eternal saving act, the extra-sacramental and sacramental life of grace form one meaningful whole in such a way that the first effects of a sacrament of desire grow from within toward the essentially sacramental encounter with Christ in which the mature perfection of the life of grace is achieved. . . .[73]

The growth of the life of grace is an historical process: in the life of every individual man, in that of each distinctive people, and of mankind as a whole. Each individual in his own time and place has his opportunities to contribute to the whole process, as does each nation; and each of the historical stages of mankind

[73] *Op. cit.,* p. 178.

may also be considered necessary elements in the gradual historical unfolding which manifests and accomplishes progressively
what God has done once through Christ for all men. The pre-
liminary elements are the necessary foundations for the subsequent events which complete historically what went before in a
meaningful whole of total achievement. But all of the events of
before and after are equally valid as the historical achievements
and manifestations of the same eternally actual saving will of
God for all men. This saving will is realized in the respective
terms and stages of history because God Himself made man in this
condition of gradual unfolding. So we may say that this "extra-
sacramental grace" is equally essential and available for the salvation of all men, whether evangelized or not yet evangelized; for
it is no less salutary than the "sacramental grace" for which it
prepares and in which it is completed and with which it forms
one single reality—necessary as well for the salvation of the
evangelized, whose sacramental life of grace in the Church is the
visible sign of salvation to become progressively manifest in the
history of all peoples for a witness of what Christ has done once
for all. Thus, the members of the sacramental community of the
Church in each nation are the visible "first fruits" of salvation
historically manifested. But they are not the only fruits.[74]

In the normal course of the historical and cultural development
of each people, the religiously significant inner instincts of men
tend toward external and community expression in certain more
or less fixed cultured forms and patterns constituting the "tribal
religion" through which the people explicitly recognize and externally signify their creaturely dependence on God and their

[74] These other fruits are called by K. Rahner "anonymous Christians,"
because "God's grace, with its power to save the world, works for the most
part anonymously." See *The Christian Commitment*, pp. 91–93.

need for His aid in the fulfillment of their communal and individual destinies; and so they offer to God the homage appropriate to their limited lights. Together with these religious expressions, there is invariably handed on from generation to generation some form of moral code as a guide to human behavior in relation to God and man. Anthropological study increasingly confirms Bergson's observation that "there has never been a society without religion."[75] The general basis for such religions is "the Word of God [Who] has never ceased to be present in the face of men,"[76] revealing Himself through the cosmos and in the consciences of men. The notion of the love of God in these culture-religions may appear inadequate when compared with this same notion in Christianity. But Christianity, we must recall, is their historical completion in "the latter days," and presupposes all that went before. Moreover, even where organized religions may be somewhat inadequate (even Christianity in certain of its historical manifestations), the human conscience remains what it is, as also the grace of God. St. Paul has strongly emphasized this. And it is especially noteworthy, with respect to all we have been saying, that the Apostle to the Nations likens the situation of the pagans living after Christ to those who lived before: never left without God's testimony,[77] manifesting Himself in the gift of life and breath and all things,[78] ever close to men groping after Him from all parts of the earth in their appointed times and places,[79] their consciences bearing witness to them.[80]

Father Jean Daniélou examines God's universal salvific will

[75] *The Two Sources of Morality and Religion,* by Henri Bergson, Doubleday, Garden City, 1954, p. 102.

[76] St. Iranaeus, *loc. cit.*   [77] Acts 14:14–17.

[78] Acts 17:25.   [79] Acts 17:26–27.

[80] Rom 2:14–15.

from this viewpoint of the witness of conscience and the pristine faith of the cosmic religion with its own "everlasting covenant,"[81] which is valid for all who have been historically unable to recognize the subsequent covenants of the old and the new Israel. Here all of the just men, who were neither Jews nor Christians, mentioned in Scripture are the historical pledge of sanctity and salvation for "that immense body of pagan humanity" (the vast majority of redeemed mankind), living both before and after Christ. They have not known Him historically in the certitude of prophecy, nor in the flesh, nor in His sacramental presence; but they have known Him "in that rectitude of desire which theology recognizes as a form of baptism."[82] "It is not without cause," wrote St. Gregory the Great, "that the life of a just pagan is set before us as a model side by side with the life of the Israelites. Our Savior, coming for the redemption of Jews and Gentiles, willed also to be foretold by Jews and Gentiles."[83] What He has foretold, He has done.

So we see how it is that God also uses for his saving purpose the various religions of men which are handed on, outside the Judeo-Christian tradition. These religions are the valid historical instruments through which communities, as well as individuals, may be disposed by God to live the life of grace. Thus, in the

---

[81] On this covenant made with Noe, see Daniélou, *op. cit.,* p. 12–13: " 'Behold I will establish my covenant with you and with your seed after you' (Gn 9:10). The object of this covenant is the promise . . . to respect the order of the cosmos: 'All the days of the earth, seedtime and harvest, cold and heat, summer and winter, night and day shall not cease' (8:22). It is eternal, irrevocable (9:16). It is a universal covenant which concerns the whole of humanity (9.6). It has for its memorial, as its sacred sign, the rainbow: 'I shall see it,' says God, 'and shall remember the everlasting covenant that was made between God and every living soul' (9:16)."

[82] Daniélou, *ibid.,* p. 4–5.

[83] Quoted by Daniélou, *ibid*.

history of salvation we see how the possibility of grace exists not only within the visible Church, and not only in the hearts of men, but also in the world of non-Christian religions.[84] For these religions are not just the results of natural reason and sin, but also of grace, which—in this existing order of redeemed mankind —"enfolds man, the sinner and the unbeliever too, as his very sphere of existence which he can never escape from."[85] In these religions, underneath whatever vagueness and distortion there may be, as a preparation and foreshadowing of what is to come to each people historically in the visible Church, inward grace is obscurely active and achieves a certain visible manifestation.[86] The basic premise of the argument, as presented by Father Schillebeeckx, is this:

that the present universal order of existence is a supernatural order. Man is created for Christ (Col. 1:16); no fully human moral orientation is possible without immediately being implicitly an orientation for or against the *Deus salutaris*. A religion founded purely on philosophical insight, "nature religion" based on that which the unaided human spirit can achieve of itself, is a fiction, metaphysically impossible in fact, because the *eidos* of religion, as phenomenologically established in the analysis of the universally human fact of religion, necessarily implies personal relations between God and man, and these clearly cannot be achieved by the created powers of man alone.

In the concrete, all religion presupposes an at least anonymous supernatural revelation and faith. There is thus, anterior to any Judeo-Christian religion, an *instinctus divinus* arising from the deepest foundations of human religious psychology as influenced by the attraction of divine grace. Thus it is that the development of rites or of "sacramentality," as an expression of, and a field of experience for, the fundamental human need to approach God, can at the same time

[84] See Rahner, *Nature and Grace,* pp. 18, 29; also the *Dogmatic Constitution on the Church,* II, 16.

[85] *Ibid.,* p. 32.

[86] See Schillebeeckx, *op. cit.,* pp. 6, 8.

and in the measure of the authenticity of the religious experience underlying it, be the manifestation of an anonymous but none the less effective operation of grace. Hence the "sacraments of nature."[87]

In keeping with a long standing tradition, St. Thomas recognized in the "sacraments of nature" a truly supernatural element, and even a concealed indication of Christ Himself.[88] This explains also the ease with which not a few of the symbols of the "nature religions" found their way into the rites and sacraments of the Church.[89] For the supernatural presupposes the natural, and finds in natural human symbols the suitable instruments for the visible manifestation of internal grace. Thus, there are found in the various non-Christian religions certain valid foreshadowings and fragments which, used by God in communicating the life of grace, constitute an "unconscious Christianity," recognized even by the early Fathers:

St. Augustine explains in a masterly manner how the service of God which we know and practice in the Church is as old as the world. He has divided the gradual coming into being of the Church in the course of human history into three great phases: the "Church" of the devout heathen; the pre-Christian phase of the Christian Church in the form of the chosen race of Israel; and finally the emergence of the mature Church, the "Church of the first born" (Heb 12:23). . . .
In a nebulous but nonetheless discernible fashion the sacramental Church is already present in the life of the whole of mankind. All humanity receives that inward word of God calling men to a union of grace with himself. . . ."[90]

This whole approach to the meaning and the means of salvation for all men, through the gradual accomplishment and mani-

[87] *Ibid.*, pp. 6–7, footnote.
[88] *Ibid.*, pp. 6–7, 9; St. Thomas: *In IV Sent.*, d. 1, q. 2, a. 6, sol. 3; *Summa Theol.*, I–II q. 103, a. 1.
[89] Schillebeeckx, *op. cit.*, p. 7.
[90] *Ibid.*, p. 5; St. Augustine: *PL* 44, cols. 161, 315, 974; *PL* 43, cols. 609–10; *Ps. 90, sermo* 2, *PL* 37, col. 1159.

festation in history of what God has done once through Christ, contains the answer to Dante's question about the man who was born on the shores of the River Indus, and lived his good life without anyone to tell him of Christ.

We must recognize [writes Teilhard de Chardin] that in the whole process which from first to last activates and directs the elements of the universe, *everything forms a single whole*. . . . For in presenting the Christian doctrine of salvation, it must not be forgotten that the world, taken as a whole, that is to say, insofar as it consists in a hierarchy of souls—which appear only successively, develop only collectively and will be completed only in union—the world, too, undergoes a sort of vast "ontogenesis" (a vast becoming what it is) in which the development of each soul, assisted by the perceptible realities on which it depends, is but a diminishing harmonic. Beneath our efforts to put spiritual form into our own lives, the world slowly accumulates, starting with the whole of matter, that which will make of it the Heavenly Jerusalem or the New Earth.[91]

[91] *Op. cit.,* pp. 32–33.

99

45635

IV.

The Nations

The people is mankind in its radical comprehensiveness.
ROMANO GUARDINI

The abstract notion of the individual has become so highly refined in the thought and so dominant in the conduct of Western man that it is sometimes difficult for him to see the movement of history and the meaning of faith through another equally valid category which is common to Scripture and familiar to the rest of the world, namely, the solidarity of human society in the dimensions of biological space-time. Bantu theologians, drawing on a fresher and more intimate experience of oneness within a clearly defined ethnic-culture group, will perhaps one day show us more fully what this means in terms of Christian life and corporate salvation. But there is much we know already. Missionary activity is directly and primarily concerned with the nations who make up mankind. This includes in one single view not only every single individual on earth today, but all who have ever lived or will live in intimate relationship with one another through the biological, cultural, and historical continuity which makes a people one. For every single person is intelligible, to himself and to others, only in relation to the particular ethnic-culture unit of people through whom he is given existence and among whom his brief time is spent. It is only within the inherited context of his tribe, his people, or his nation, that each one

100

works out his final salvation together with all the others. No man goes alone to God.[1]

We may analyze salvation in terms of God's action in a man's heart and in man's individual response through grace. But we must recall that this salvation is essentially a corporate affair already achieved once for all men collectively, although it is tangibly brought to bear on each one only through the gradual unfolding of history, in which each event (including the establishment of the visible Church among a particular people) has its appointed time, and every man (whether living before or after the sacramental advent of Christ in His visible Church among His own particular people) has his moments of freedom and of grace. The salvation of all those who are finally saved among any people is being historically externalized and completed through the sacramental presence of Christ in the Church, which is destined by her very nature to become once for all in each nation what she is: the universal sign of salvation, achieving the full significance throughout the world of Christ's redeeming presence among all men, doing sacramentally among one people after another what He has already done historically once for all—and what He does eternally in the souls of all who are saved. Therefore, all who are finally saved in any nation or tribe or people are members of the Church, whether or not they lived before or after the time of Christ's sacramentally saving presence among their

[1] One well known example of corporate acts of this kind is the Christian practice of infant Baptism, where the child's personal intention is not in virtue of his own individually personal act, but in virtue of the community of faith into which he is born, and in virtue of the explicit acts of those who present him for Baptism; see St. Thomas, *Summa Theol.*, III, q. 68, a. 9, ad 1. See also the *Dogmatic Constitution on the Church,* November 21st, 1964, chapter 2, no. 9: "God does not make men holy and save them merely as individuals . . ."

own people; they belong to Christ either visibly or invisibly, either consciously or unconsciously.[2]

The progressive extension of the visible Church among one after another of the peoples who make up mankind signifies sacramentally in time and place the historically developing Parousia, which is eternal in origin and efficacy, and which was introduced into concrete human history at Bethlehem, and which shall again be manifest in historical tangibility at the end of history when every eye shall see Christ in the fullness and the glory of the final Parousia. But this will be only after the visible Church on earth shall have made Christ sacramentally present once for all in every nation; only after the Church shall have accomplished her earthly mission of bringing about a corporate confrontation (including therein every individual encounter) between the redeeming Christ and the peoples who constitute the whole of mankind. The end will not come until the Gospel shall *first* have been preached for a witness among every people.[3] So we are led to a consideration of the meaning of human solidarity, through which corporate salvation is achieved, in terms of the scriptural, historical, and anthropological category called "the nations," or "the peoples"—that is to say, in terms of mankind in the concrete diversity of ethnic-culture (but not necessarily political) units of men. Then we must relate this notion to what we understand by the "salvation of men," in order finally to see how the history of mankind's salvation is gradually realized and brought to completion through the missionary activity of the visible Church seek-

[2] This notion of "unconscious" Christians is explained in the previous chapter: the "Anonymous Christians" whose historical condition makes it possible for them to attain only the "extra-sacramental" life of grace. See also Vonier, *op. cit.,* p. 122.

[3] Mk 13:10; Mt 24:14.

ing to establish herself as a living reality among each distinctive "people."

Christ is the light of nations; and the visible Church is Christ becoming sacramentally tangible to all nations in the extension of time and place until all of the families of men shall have been sacramentally gathered into the saving unity which the Church's universal mission signifies and accomplishes *re-presentatively*. This recurring theme of Scripture marks both the begining and the end, and indeed permeates the whole, of the Second Vatican Council's *Dogmatic Constitution on the Church*. Our understanding of the Church's historical mission is, therefore, determined in a very fundamental way by the theological significance which attaches to these ethnic-culture units of men. Who are these "tribes" and "tongues" and "peoples" and "nations," and how are they defined sociologically with reference to the Church's activity of gathering from among them the new people of God? Finally, what do these ethnological categories mean in relation to mankind's corporate destiny, and in relation to the Church's *raison d'être?*

These questions are elementary. But they are not easy to answer without at the same time raising a whole new series of complex questions which could be adequately answered only by a theologically oriented study of the social sciences, psychology, and history. In general, however, we can define what we mean by "the people" or "the nations"—and such a definition is offered in the third part of this chapter—and we can also discern the significance of this category as the real and as the symbolic material through which the Church becomes progressively the universal sign of the unity and the salvation of all men. Yet in each concrete instance of preaching the Gospel or of establishing the Church for a witness among this or that people, we must evaluate this or that community in the light of our definition and in the light of what we hope to achieve. In each case, we must ask ourselves whether or not this particular ethnic-culture group is truly a people apart in the community of mankind, and whether or not they have already been evangelized. We would also have to decide about the real possibility of achieving our missionary goals among them, at least in some measure. Otherwise, we may end up by concentrating our missionary resources in the wrong places, while ignoring and neglecting more realistic possibilities in other fields. For, as Paul VI has reminded us, the opportunities for evangelization among peoples may pass, never to return.[4] It is a matter of organizing the Church's missionary activity according to theological principles, a matter of establishing a priority which is related to historically attainable goals among the nations in our time.

1. The Solidarity of Mankind

Human destiny is achieved only corporately. Man's life is lived and his personality is fulfilled only in community. This is a primary fact of human existence. It is, therefore, only in terms of unity that individuals may find salvation. We have some understanding, at least some experiential knowledge, of the solidarity of a human family with its inheritance rooted immediately and obviously in biology. We also believe in the solidarity of mankind, the all-embracing human family with its more remote and less obvious unity of stock. We believe in the universal brotherhood of all men in the flesh: Adam is the father of us all, and Christ is our brother. We have all fallen

[4] From Paul VI's address on the canonization of the twenty-two Uganda martyrs, October 18th, 1964.

in Adam, and we are all lifted up in Christ Who is our brother in the flesh because He is the son of David and therefore also, like ourselves, a son of Adam. Scripture often uses the name "Adam" to designate the whole of mankind collectively, as well as to designate one man individually. It is the same with Christ. He is the one God-Man Who appeared once in history, but also He is each and all who believe in Him.[5] He is even one with those who have not yet believed.[6] For, indeed, He is the Second Adam.[7]

We are familiar with the notion of one single individual chosen to represent some group or other, to stand for the whole, to intercede for the rest, and even to decide certain aspects of their corporate destiny. This individual may lead his whole group well or badly; he may influence all for good or for ill. But the unity under one head in this case is merely moral. The group may, therefore, replace this individual with someone else. It is not the same with Adam and with Christ. They represent all men because they are all men in a metaphysical unity, preëxistent to any moral unity. Yet, because of man's free and incommunicable nature within the community of fallen and redeemed mankind, there is room for individual as well as collective guilt, for individual as well as corporate acts of salvation. Within the framework of his historically conditioned community, each man may or may not make his personal contributions to the destiny of the whole; and each may, in his positive contributions, represent and

[5] Jn 17:22–23; Eph 4:16; Col 1:18.

[6] Pius XII: "We should recognize in other men, although they are not yet joined to us in the Body of the Church, our brothers according to the flesh, called, together with us, to the same eternal salvation." *Mystici Corporis,* NCWC translation, Washington, D.C., 1943, no. 96, p. 37.

[7] Rom 5:12–21; 1 Cor 15:22–23. See *Corporate Personality in Ancient Israel,* by H. W. Robinson, Fortress, Philadelphia, 1964.

be the whole. For the whole is its members, and the members are the whole.

The man who has understood [in the words of Romano Guardini], that every self exists also in his neighbor; that every man shares the life of all other men, and that his happiness and suffering are bound up with theirs, will realize that, in the dogma of original sin, the Church has really touched the very foundations of all human society. . . .

It is this very solidarity which makes the community of redemption possible. Since every man in his profoundest being is bound up with his fellows, so that another's guilt can become his, the atonement made by the One can be the atonement made by all the rest. . . . Jesus became our representative, and His sufferings thus became the property of our race. He redeemed us, not by His example, doctrine or instruction—all these are of secondary importance—but by the representative and atoning satisfaction in which He assumed before God the responsibility of our guilt.[8]

This solidarity embraces all of mankind: those living before as well as after Christ in His historical presence and in His sacramental presence. "So far reaching is this objective community of atonement that, by its power, any child, without any coöperation on its part, is reborn into a new life and mode of existence."[9]

This oneness of all men was better understood by the early Fathers of the Church than it is today. St. Gregory of Nyssa was able to set forth this truth with a directness and ease which we have long since lost:

When Scripture says that God created man, this indefinite expression "man" means "*universal human nature*." . . . The creature is called man—not any particular man, but man in general. This general term, used for the nature created, indicates that God in His foreknowledge included the whole human race in this first fashioning. . . . The

[8] *The Church and the Catholic and the Spirit of the Liturgy,* by Romano Guardini, Sheed & Ward, New York, 1935, pp. 101–102.

[9] *Ibid.,* p. 102.

gracious gift of likeness to God was not given to a mere section of humanity, to one individual man; no, it is a perfection which finds its way in equal measure to every member of the human race. . . . On this score, there is no difference between the first man that ever was and the last man that will be: All bear the stamp of divinity. Thus the whole of humanity was named as one man, since for the Divine Power there is neither past nor future. . . . The whole human nature, then, from the first man to the last, is but one image of Him Who is. . . .

God said, "Let us make man to our image and likeness." This image of God finds its fulfillment in human nature as a whole. . . . By "man," then, is meant the universal nature of man, this God-like thing, made in the likeness of God. It was not a mere part of the whole that came into being through the all-powerful wisdom of God, but the whole extension of the created nature at once.[10]

In like manner, St. Augustine wrote:

Now Adam's name, as I have said more than once, means . . . the whole world. . . . Set in one place, he fell and, as it were, broken small, he has filled the whole world. But the Divine Mercy gathered up the fragments from every side. . . . He Who refashioned was Himself the fashioner.[11]

Because our faith postulates the preëxisting metaphysical unity of all men in the first and in the Second Adam, there is a temptation to approach the mystery of corporate salvation in the light only of this lofty truth, without going into the question of the "natural" and lesser unities of men. This approach, as proposed by Abbot Vonier, seems to offer an easy solution to the missionary question:

It is an *a priori* possibility, which I think we can all admit, that God is able to make provision in the supernatural sphere for the whole of mankind through one select part of mankind, that privileged portion

[10] *On the Formation of Man, PG* 44, chapter 16, nos. 181–185; chapter 22, nos. 204–205; quoted in *Catholicism,* by Henri de Lubac, S.J., Sheed & Ward, New York, 1950, pp. 210–211.

[11] *On Ps.* 95, no. 15, *PL* 37, 1236; quoted by de Lubac, *ibid.,* p. 234.

which is directly and unmistakably sanctified, and in which is found the fullness of grace, the fullness of intercessory power, and the fullness of apostolic works. From this sanctified core of humanity there would proceed an endless current of supernatural magnetism which would leave no one untouched or unenergized.

In such an hypothesis, whatever salvation there is in the world at large would come directly through the Church, so that the presence of the Church *on earth* would be the supreme mercy for the human race, not only for the actual members of the Church, but for the whole of mankind. . . . I do not think that anyone could doubt God's power to leaven the world with supernatural life through a definite institution such as the Church.

It is my own opinion that the Catholic Church actually holds the position which I have described as an hypothesis."

This is a profound and enlightening observation, so far as it goes. It shows us how a body of men, who would actually be a minority in relation to the totality of human kind, are corporately saved even though—because of radical social changes in certain parts of the world and in different historical periods—they may have become, as it were, "de-tribalized" or cut off from their progenitors; and these progenitors will thus have ceased to exist as a distinctive people in their progeny. This de-tribalized body of men may not be identified with any particular ethnic-culture unit of people for whom, in their history, the Church has been or will be the indigenously erected sign of salvation, their corporate salvation is nevertheless accomplished by Christ in mankind's history, and signified sacramentally by the Church's catholic presence to mankind. Abbot Vonier's credible hypothesis is, however, incomplete. It might even tempt us to a sort of "quietism" as regards the urgency of missionary activity directed to the peoples among whom the *Lumen Gentium* has not yet appeared sacramentally in the Church firmly established among them.

[12] *Op. cit.,* p. 121–123; italics added.

What must also be considered—and this will demonstrate the validity of Vonier's basic insight—is the relationship of this hypothesis to the concrete historical situation of man as he is actually scattered over the earth in those distinctive ethnic-culture units which Scripture calls "the nations," and to which the Church's missionary activity is specifically directed. Vonier is not the only one who seems to have overlooked the missionary significance of this natural category of men: the *ethnei* of Scripture, the *ethnici* of the mission encyclicals, the "peoples" of the social sciences.

Father Schillebeeckx also seems to avoid the real difficulty by considering the missionary task as directed to "pagan cultures" rather than to nations or peoples.[13] And Father Rahner, who still wonders about the theological correctness of regarding parts of Europe as mission countries,[14] has nevertheless developed his very interesting Diaspora thesis without any mention of the missionary and scriptural significance of the nations. He tells us that the Gospel has already been preached "to a certain measure . . . all over the world," and that the Church "has begun to be in actuality world-wide." So, "Christianity (though in very varying proportions) exists everywhere in the world, and everywhere as a Diaspora."[15] The careful word "everywhere" is perhaps sufficient to justify Father Rahner's thesis, as this might mean every continent merely—still leaving much room for discussion. But Scripture speaks of "every tribe and tongue and people and nation." Certainly, the *Lumen Gentium* has not yet been manifested among all of these *gentes* by the relatively insignificant number of Christian missionaries who have been trying to achieve

[13] From his personal letter to the author, February 22nd, 1964.
[14] *The Christian Commitment,* p. 25.
[15] *Ibid.,* pp. 25–29.

this goal. In any case, the primary function of the Church's messianic mission is not directed to every place, in the sense of continents or geographical localities; nor is it directed to every nation, considered as a political unit; rather, it is directed to every people or nation, taken in the sense of ethnic-culture units of men. Thus, it is not a matter of here or there or even everywhere; it is not a matter of geography merely.

The metaphysical unity of mankind in Adam and in Christ is the ultimate basis of corporate salvation. But this is not yet a visible solidarity. It will be such only at the end. In the meantime, the unfolding history of salvation gradually manifests this invisible reality only through the lesser forms of human solidarity, which are tangible and intelligible signs of the unity and final reconciliation of all things. The total unity of all is only progressively achieved in the course of history; but this unity is based on what is natural and already existing in visible human forms which are both relevant to a man in his personal experience, and significant to him in his common understanding of himself as a social being in a particular historical context. The *ultimate* unity of all men is normally outside of man's common psychological experience, although it may be glimpsed occasionally in a fleeting and intuitive fashion through certain profound human experiences. In the realm of aesthetics, for example, one may think of the transient vision-feeling communicated by a great painting or symphony. But this kind of experience is not an everyday psychological event for most men. This sense of human solidarity does not come to most men as casually and connaturally as it does in the many concrete and mundane events through which we experience our oneness and common destiny within a sharply defined "people"; and this is especially true in the non-Western world, where the inner meaning of "the people" has not yet been lost.

For the common awareness of human solidarity, which is quite real, we must look to the unity of "the tribe," or "the people." It is here, where it is actually lived in tangible history, that the abstract notion of our essentially social existence and corporate destiny has its roots in human experience and its relevance for most men. Here is the natural basis for that final unity of mankind which is achieved not in terms of isolated individuals, but in terms of peoples. Here we find the psychologically relevant manifestation of the invisible unity toward which we tend in Christ. Here we see the meaning of the scriptural "nations." To discuss the mission of the Church without considering the significance of "the nations," would be like talking about the nature of Baptism without mentioning the meaning of water. For the completion of the messianic mission, and therefore of the Church's ministry of reconciliation,[16] is to be viewed primarily in the light of "the nations" flocking together under the signal, the *Lumen Gentium,* beckoning to the peoples all around.[17] Let Christ *first* be made known sacramentally to every people, and *then* shall He come in glory.[18]

2. Symbolized in "The People"

Between the obvious solidarity of the members of a single family unit and the invisible unity of mankind as a whole there exist many other unities of men united to one another by bonds which

[16] 2 Cor 5:18–19.
[17] Is. 11:10–13; 42:4–7; 55:5; Mt 12:18–21; Acts 13:47; Tim 4:17; Ap 1:7; 5:9; 7:9, to cite only a few texts.
[18] Mk 13:10; Mt 24:14.

are more or less recognizable. Between the smallest and the largest units, of the family and of mankind respectively, there is a whole hierarchy of groupings. There is the extended family of grandparents, uncles, aunts, cousins, etc. However separate in many ways its members may be, they are all one in the mysterious and often immediately conscious unity of biology in the manifestations of its most intimate function of generation. In the wider circle of the more extended families, there are the clans which have lost their conscious meaning, if not their existence, in the more homogeneous societies of certain parts of the world. And in the ever widening circle there are the tribes (often including subtribes) whose members see themselves, and are recognized by others, as *a people apart* in the greater community of mankind. While this notion of the tribe may have been lost through the greater coalescence of men in many places, it remains, nevertheless, a singularly intelligible and natural unit for countless millions of men (and perhaps for the majority of mankind considered in its totality) who regard themselves primarily, if not exclusively, in terms of "the tribe." In the hierarchy of human unities, this may be taken as the smallest natural unit of men who are in their own eyes, and in the estimation of their neighbors, distinct from all "the others." In their own experience of social self-awareness, they are preëminently "the people." The remainder of mankind is "the others."

Among the so-called "primitive" peoples—who are just as far away from human origins as are all of their contemporaries—this corporate self-awareness is often quite naked: or shall we say, more natural and therefore more human. For example, a large group of pastoral inhabitants of northern Uganda calls itself "Karamojong," which means literally "the original people." But the distinction between "the people" (or "ourselves") and "the others" is made by men not along tribal lines only; it may also be made to include a number of originally different peoples or tribes who have evolved historically into a greater unity. So "the people" may even become coterminous with a political-economic unit of varied ethnic-culture origins, although in such instances this kind of self-awareness might not be so acutely conscious. Likewise, the historical divisions of a single ethnic-culture group may give birth to new peoples who come to see themselves mutually as *a people apart* from one another. Thus, the validity of this notion of "the people" rests on the practical historical judgment of those concerned and of their neighbors. The relative absence of this manifestation of man's essentially social nature and destiny in Western thought and conduct is not necessarily a sign of human progress and advancement. But a radical reëvaluation, by philosophers and theologians and statesmen, of our once-dominant and now largely retrenched individualism, suggests that we are laboriously re-discovering what we really are; and this, notwithstanding the fact that extreme individualism is making a last-ditch stand in certain quarters under the thin guise of philosophical existentialism, ecclesiastical conservatism, and political escapism.

What is being rediscovered in the Western world, and has perhaps never been lost to the rest of the world, is the meaning of "the people" as the "primary association of human beings who by race, country, and historical antecedents share the same life and destiny," as Guardini describes it. He continues:

The people is a human society which maintains an unbroken continuity with the roots of nature and life, and obeys their intrinsic laws.
The people contains—not numerically or quantitatively, but in essential unity—the whole of mankind, in all its human variety of ages,
sexes, temperament, mental and physical condition; to which must be
added the sum total of its works and spheres of production as de-

termined by class and vocation. The people is mankind in its radical comprehensiveness."[19]

And, we must add, it is only in terms of his own people that any man is able to comprehend his real solidarity with the whole of mankind; not only comprehend it, but realize it in his meaningful behavior. For "the people" is to its own members the symbolic body of mankind, visibly signifying to each man the invisible solidarity of all men. It is only in this perspective that we can see the full significance of the Church's missionary activity, and the authentic implications of the much-abused maxim, "Charity begins at home"—with "begins" as the dynamic word in this new perspective.

While many distinctive peoples may in the course of time merge into one people, and one people may split into many, the missionary function of the Church is concerned with the here-and-now existing situation of this time and place in which the whole Church is called to make herself visibly present, as a firmly rooted witness among the particular peoples for whom this sign of their salvation has not yet been raised up. Christ did not wait for mankind to become one in the visible tangibility of history, through the external evolutionary forces of man-made politics and economics, before embarking on His historical mission. Despite the apparent unity of all peoples, which the Western nations might appear to be creating under the aegis of technology, we are not yet on the verge of that grand unification of humanity which will entitle us to regard all previous history and human experience as mere steppingstones to that moment.

We should not have to be reminded that all of the peoples of the past and of the future, as well as our contemporaries who have not yet succumbed to the real or imagined (we do not yet know

[19] *Op. cit.*, p. 9.

114

which) hegemony of the Western world, are all ends in themselves and worlds unto themselves with equally valid, even if accidentally different, experiences of human existence. Each person and every people starts again and lives afresh the essentially same experience, requiring nothing from us for the attainment of their mundane fullness of life, as Herbert Butterfield has said so well. Nor should we have to be told again that the full taste of life is available even to those who know nothing of our art and philosophy and technology. To be sure, we all have something special which others have not, but we all lack much more than we have:

The whole human race together may compass a great range of knowledge, experience and capacities; but all these are terribly broken and splintered between all of the individuals that go to compose the race; and all of us lack a multitude of those things which the liberal would regard as essential to a complete man or a completely rounded view of life. . . . Each of us is more or less restricted to a narrow vision, gravely conditioned by time, temperament, and age, and by the platform on which we happen to be standing.[20]

Therefore, when we hear our Catholic contemporaries telling us that the most serious problem in the world today is the rapid spread of atheism, or that the greatest danger to the Church today is "the loss of the working class," we must remember that what they are talking about is their own world of Europe and the Americas in the first case, and the world of France and Belgium in the second. Among the remaining two-thirds or more of mankind, these are not the great problems at all.

All men are equally distant from eternity, and equally close; all are made and saved by the same Father Who is untrammeled by the times and places of the historical sojourn common to all who are

[20] *Christianity and History,* by Herbert Butterfield, Scribner's, New York, 1950, p. 118.

interrelated to one another with the equal necessity of each note in a symphony. The work of the composer and of the orchestra is no mere sequence of notes and bars leading up, through sounds of ever increasing beauty, to a fullness which shall be achieved only in the final bar. The beauty and fullness of all, as with the meaning of life on earth, is always and everywhere in the now of each sound which alone touches eternity, but only as a part of the whole in and for which it exists. So the achievements of our particular times and places have their aspect of eternal significance. But on their externally measurable side, which always appears more striking to us, they are quite ephemeral. Later ages may well consider the present extension of Western influence as nothing more than a short-lived historical phenomenon with perhaps even less universality and permanence than the grand edifices built by ancient Christendom on the ruins of the Roman Empire. We really do not care to think much about the judgment of history which is already on us, for we know that "the sentence falls on great human systems, on nations, civilizations, institutions; indeed on all the schematized patterns into which human life ranges itself in various periods. The systems break, the organizations crumble. . . ."[21] What remains always, and with an essential sameness, is the people everywhere.

The external unity of peoples within a political state or a superstate (providing all with one artificial culture and value system), considered in the light of mankind's total history and common destiny, has, therefore, nothing more to do with the inner reality of the messianic Kingdom than the present-day political experiment of the Israeli State has to do with the return of the "chosen remnant" of Israel's sons to the New Jerusalem. The real unity

[21] *Ibid.,* p. 87.

of men, and the only lasting kingdom, is "within"; and it is among all peoples of every time and place. This has no essential dependence on any "kingdom," ecclesiastical or otherwise, made by some men and offered to all the others. The only authentic reunion of mankind is that which God initiates and accomplishes in the hearts of men through Christ, Who brings it to visibly signified completion in His Church as she progressively, if sometimes sluggishly, becomes in historical extension what she is: the sacramental *Lumen Gentium*.

The Church, therefore, insofar as she is God's instrument for realizing the messianic mission in its visibly signified historical extension, has the primary function of showing and accomplishing symbolically the unique unity of all peoples, and the very meaning of all history. Indeed, as we have seen, this is her fundamental mission, to manifest Christ for and among one people after another in His sacramental Parousia, calling to explicit faith and hope and love the visible witnesses, who are chosen from eternity out of every tribe and tongue and people, to stand symbolically (sacramentally) with Christ among all men, until this sacramental manifestation converges at the culmination point of history in the final Parousia of Christ returned again in His now-glorified historical tangibility at the end of all history. The sacramental advent of Christ among all peoples is the necessary means and the essential preparation for His historical return in glory, as St. Bernard reminds us in his fifth sermon for Advent:

In the first advent, He comes in the flesh and in weakness; in the second, He comes in spirit and in power; in the third, He comes in glory and in majesty.

And the second coming is the means whereby we pass from the first to the third.

Scripture has much to say about the nations, especially in reference to the historical mission of the Messiah. There is a striking unity of thought in these texts which, taken together, show us the meaning of missionary activity in the Church; for the Church continues sacramentally this one mission of Christ. He is the signal beckoning to all peoples among whom He is to become the sign of their salvation; calling His elect, who are still a scattered remnant among the tribes and tongues and peoples, to form the new and eschatological Israel for a witness to all men in every nation.[22] Can we avoid the missionary significance of these "tribes and tongues and peoples and nations"? These are the valid historical and anthropological categories in which the vast majority of men have always found themselves quite naturally, and in which they have their immediate experience of human solidarity before God and in relation to other men.

So the Gospel message of the New Covenant is directed specifically to the nations out of whom the chosen disciples are called by the historically evident sacramental presence of Christ in His historically established community of explicit faith and tangible Christian witness, extending from Jerusalem to the ends of the earth, and destined to be present once for all among each people at some time in their respective histories. The fact that some peoples have ceased to exist without the visible Church having ever been historically present among them, or the possibility that some peoples may reject this presence even up to the end, does not mean that the Church has not been present to them in the invisible presence of unconscious (or "anonymous") Christians; nor would this diminish the validity of the Church as a universal symbol of mankind's total unity; for a sacramental

22 Is 24:13–16; 49:6; 52:15; 60:4–6; 66:18–21; Ps 71:17–18; Acts 13:47; 15:14; Rom 1:5, 15, 18; 11:5–8, to cite only a few texts.

118

sign, which is what the visible Church is among the nations, is not a numerically quantitative representation of the signified reality. It is simply a symbol: enough of the reality itself adequately to convey the meaning to men. Thus, the notion of corporate salvation in Christ is psychologically and historically verified by the Church among the nations. It is verified in symbolic visibility for some men (conscious Christians) whose sacramental lives, whose explicit faith and hope and love, signify externally the presence within them of saving grace; not within them alone, but also within all the others (unconscious Christians) whose response to grace has been or shall be merely internal because of the particular historical context which Providence assigns them. But for them also, the Church, extended in history among different peoples in different times and varied places, is the same universal sign of salvation and of reconciliation.

While he was not dealing specifically with the missionary significance of the nations, Guardini has nevertheless discerned the most important aspect of the question under consideration here, and the very conclusion toward which we are tending:

God takes possession of mankind as such, of the unity, welded by all the biological, geographical, cultural, and social ties which bind one human being to others; that mysterious unity which, though composed entirely of individuals, is more than their sum total.

If this whole is to be laid hold upon by God, it is not necessary that all men should be numerically included in it. It is sufficient that God's grace should take hold of the community as such, that something which transcends the individual. This, however, can be accomplished in a small *representative* group.[23]

In essence, this is the same as Vonier's insight cited above. If we relate this notion of community to "the nations" as we have been considering them, then immediately we see the fundamental mis-

[23] *Op. cit.,* p. 34; italics added.

sionary significance of the different "peoples." We see how the few who are chosen—and who are called out of every people to form the visible Church in each nation—*represent* sacramentally all among their own people and all of mankind collectively, all, that is, who have from the beginning to the end responded invisibly to God's universal offer of saving grace.

3. The Divisions of Mankind

The present divisions of the peoples of the world into separate and distinctive units started not as a punishment, but as a normal historical movement in harmony with the natural increase of the human population. As an obvious dictate of nature, this is a manifestation of God's will: "The ruler of all has divided the nations apart . . . giving each people its own home."[24] The people of Nimrod were, "by the grace of God," huntsmen.[25] The other families of men developed their characteristic traits in relation to the various biological and geographical regions into which their search for a place to settle brought them. We know, by this time, that it is not due to any kind of divine punishment that one people is different from another in culture, philosophy, language, technique, and even in physique. It is rather by reason of their isolation from one another that differences naturally arose, as each separate group with the same human substratum sought subsistence and happiness in the varied ecological environments in which it found itself, and to which it was forced to make specialized and peculiar adaptations of the human genius common to all.

So it was, as we read in the Book of Genesis, that "the peoples

[24] Dt 32:8; Acts 17:26–27. [25] Gn 11:9.

spread this way and that . . . divided according to their peoples and races; and this was how the nations were scattered over the face of the earth."[26] This is appropriate to the historical condition of fallen mankind whose return to God is through time and place. It is neither a sign of any innate human perversity, nor an effect of divine wrath. The story of the Tower of Babel, with its subsequent punishment in the form of confusion of tongues and division of peoples, suggests only that any man-made attempts to form "a great people, all one," is apt to come up abruptly against the laws of nature and disconcertingly against the will of God, Who, as we know from the sequel of the latter days, has His own way of forming this "great people, all one." Each separate community, with its own particular problems of life and subsistence, has developed its own characteristic variations of language, philosophy, religion, and technology in approaching its respective problems. The sum total of all of these differences, developed by countless generations of men scattered over the face of the earth, is the historical reality of the distinctive ethnic-culture units of people who make up mankind. In each of these bold departures, giving birth to distinctive peoples, there is the hand of Providence; but there is also the proper mystique of each nation, protecting its people and telling them how to live. And there is, in each of these separate cultural developments, a unique reflection of the one goodness and truth and beauty.

Anthropologists nowadays tend to classify the peoples of the world according to linguistic families. Neat classifications might also be made according to cranial structure, or hairiness, or body odor, or diet, or any number of such things—depending on what one wishes to demonstrate. We have all of us seen the mad results of arbitrary theorizing along the lines of race and color. And

[26] Gn 9:20; 10:32.

because of this choice in classification, there is today an understandable feeling of uneasiness at any discussion of the differences between the various tribes and tongues and peoples who make up mankind. But the differences are present in the form of empirical data which we cannot ignore in our search for some deeper understanding of ourselves. So the heinous connotations given to such words as "race" and "people" in the philosophical menagerie of the Third Reich, however grim and fresh in our memories, should not put us off from seeking their authentic meanings. With due apologies for this aspect of our "civilization," we simply must say a bit more about the differences between us.

The diversities found among the peoples of the world would seem to be the result of isolated or partially isolated human communities, existing for countless generations while progressively working out their own thought and behavior patterns in their respective environments; within such communities, some of the more notable groups and individual actions constitute an historical frame of reference which, together with the gradually evolved culture patterns, forms a unique synthesis in which each element and each individual has proper meaning only in relation to the whole. Just as each distinctive language is able to say things which cannot be adequately translated into any other language, nor even be fully understood outside of the original cultural context, so also no single person would be truly intelligible even to himself if considered in isolation from the group to which he belongs. Indeed, the very notion of person, taken in the highest and absolute sense in which it is used of the Blessed Trinity, is itself essentially a relationship within a community. The person never stands alone, but always and only with an essential relationship to his own community.

And what is this community? It is any one of the distinctive ethnic-culture units which make up mankind. It is a group of men naturally united by the desire of living together—and sharing a sense of biological, geographical, cultural, and linguistic solidarity based on common traditions, problems, characteristics, and aspirations, as well as on a sense of common destiny. All of these qualities make a group of persons recognizable to themselves and to others as a people apart in the larger community of mankind.[27]

Outside of some such group, the individual is psychologically lost. He is like a man without a personality. This is why the cultural breakdown of any society is characterized by the anarchic and inhuman behavior of individuals who need the protection and pedagogy of a concrete culture. For every man sees and acts humanly only through that particular culture which is the unique and collective creation of generations of his forebears. And this cultural context gives each man his own tangible place in the total unity of mankind. Without such community experience, the notion of mankind's solidarity in Christ would be as meaningless as would be the idea of loving God to a man who had never loved another human being. All of this adds up to the fundamental truth that every single person is psychologically able to confront the real events of history only from within the context and the style of life of the group in which he is immersed and which transcends him. So the salutary event of the redeeming Christ is presented to "the nations," and we begin to see the profound significance of this scriptural category of man.

If one adopts this approach to the meaning of the "the nations," one cannot say that any single people is better than another. The

[27] The formulation of this concept owes much to *National Patriotism in the Papal Teachings,* by Bishop John J. Wright, Fides, Notre Dame, especially p. 47.

most that one can say, when he seeks to look at the rest of the
world from outside his own cultural context, is that one people
is different from another. While a particular people may excel
in one or another aspect of being human, such limited achievement can never make one group essentially better than another.
It will be found that some other people excels in something else,
and that there is always much sameness just below the various
cultural surfaces. By the very fact of excelling in one field, a
people necessarily limits itself in another. For example, by concentrating their human genius primarily on the formidable task
of surviving in a thoroughly inhospitable habitat, the people of
the Turkana Tribe of northern Kenya have up to now forfeited
many possible initiatives with regard to what lies outside their
desert environment. But they are not thereby inferior people. Far
from it. Theirs is a notable achievement of the human spirit. Nor
would one say, by the same token, that a very talented and robust
group of Oxford graduates were inferior men because they could
not survive for a year in the Turkana Desert on an equal footing
with the average tribesman.

We no longer imagine that the peoples of the less highly organized or less mechanized societies are any less human than *homo
occidentalis mechanicus*. We are all equally distant from our
beginnings, and also much nearer to those beginnings than we
like to think. While much persevering mental exercise went into
the production of the radio, we would not say that a man who
has one and knows how to turn it on is any brighter or more
humanly developed than the man who has never seen one. We
know now how much the myth of superior peoples was dependent on the Maxim gun. Little reflection is needed to realize
that the inventor of the bow and arrow was a greater genius than
the man who made the first machine gun. The latter, like the

inventor of the radio, had more knowledge on which to exercise his inventive talents. His particular time and place was subject to the vast phenomenon of cultural exchange through which the creative genius of many different peoples was put at his service, after having been handed down and improved by countless generations of thinking men in various parts of the world. As Clyde Kluckhohn remarks:

The achievements of Einstein rest upon a substructure built up by at least 5,000 years of collective effort. The theory of relativity traces its genealogy from an unknown hunter who discovered abstract numbers by notching his stick, from Mesopotamian priests and traders who invented multiplication and division, from Greek philosophers and Moslem mathematicians.[28]

Most of Western knowledge is still unknown to the Masai tribesmen of East Africa; for, up to now, they have managed to live outside the historical mainstream of cultural exchange; and, for reasons best known to themselves, they have chosen generally to ignore most of the changes impinging upon them from the outside world. Their society is interested in persons and livestock, not things. And we are all forced to concede that what counts most, in terms of the good life and genuine human progress, is not money or the rewards of technology, but the subtle refinements of simple and universal human values.

It is in the most commonplace actions and attitudes of men that the cultural originality of peoples and the real progress of the human spirit, in its multitudinous variations, shines through most splendidly. An outsider visiting the people of the Masai Tribe might, for example, be shocked at the "primitive crassness" of these people who would not think of expressing a word of gratitude after the enjoyment of generous hospitality. But a

[28] *Mirror for Man,* Fawcett, New York, 1957, p. 49.

closer acquaintance with the Masai social patterns, developed according to the exigencies of a nomadic way of life, would show that these people have such a highly refined and mutually comprehensive practice of hospitality that a word of thanks would be meaningless to them; and they themselves would be quite appalled at the limited hospitality practiced elsewhere.

Languages provide many more examples of the unique genius of each people in dealing with certain situations and notions in the face of which outsiders are apt to be quite deaf or mute or blind. So we may say with Jean Daniélou that "every race and every tongue gives expression to some irreplaceable aspect of humanity."[29] These are "the riches of the nations" which the prophets of Israel saw "pouring in upon" the new Israel, together with the elect called from among the peoples, signifying the unity of all in Christ, and tangibly fulfilling the catholic nature of the Church. These are the many colored threads to be visibly woven into the robe of the Bride,[30] making herself ready to receive her Beloved when He comes in glory at the end. But His coming is delayed until she is ready.

The Bride is being made ready through missionary activity directed to the peoples who have not yet been evangelized once, who have not yet seen the sign of their salvation raised up among them, who have not yet had the opportunity of offering their cultural riches to her. This is an eschatological function of the Church, who herself belongs to mankind's history and therefore moves toward the fulfillment of her mission with that same irreversibility which characterizes the historical human condition. Here men and events appear only successively, develop only collectively, and are completed only in the same final goal for

---

[29] *The Lord of History,* Regnery, Chicago, 1958, p. 58.
[30] Ps 44:14–15.

which all things are made, and in which all are reconciled with a renewed and transcendent meaning.

Christian history moves, not in circles revolving perpetually around select segments of humanity, but unilaterally and organically and eschatologically through all at once, from the Alpha to the Omega who is the same Lord of all.[31] In His sight, there is neither before nor after. The first are the last and the last are first, for mankind is called as one. Each historical event, even as the life of every person and of all peoples, unfolds gradually within the continuity of a single organism in the process of becoming what it is; so all that went before is no less valid than what is and what shall be. Thus, each distinctive people—even if unknown to all others—makes its own unique and progressive contribution towards the developing Kingdom of God which is invisible, in the hearts of men, before and after becoming visibly signified in the Church historically established once for all among one people after another.

The Church on earth, then, has the mission of recapitulating all in one visible symbol of unity which is herself: the Kingdom actually coming in historical tangibility to all peoples, actually making herself present in forms which are indigenous and intelligible to all. Like God, she cannot favor the mighty peoples of this world who seem to have achieved great works. For man's labor determines nothing in relation to God. The sons of Cain built the first city. But it was from among the wandering herdsmen, like Abel, that God's own people were called. Nor were they chosen from among the most "advanced" of the sons of Sem. God formed His people out of an abject and despised crowd of Bedouin nomads who had been cast by the roadside, as an unwanted infant, neither washed nor covered, but pleasing only to

[31] Ap 21:6; Acts 10:36.

127

God and made beautiful by Him for a whole world to see.[32] Nor were they chosen for "surpassing numbers," for "they were the fewest of any people."[33] So also, the chosen people of the new Israel are called from "every tribe and tongue and people," however small or insignificant or unwashed they may appear to the eyes of this world.

Is this what the Church is doing today?

[32] Ez 16:3–14.   [33] Dt 7:7.

V.

The Messianic Witness

*She is a gathering of men among other gatherings of men, but bear-
ing among them the mystery of Jesus Christ. She is the company of
witnesses to him . . . She brings Christ to the world, offering it opportunities to recognize him as the key to its destiny.*

YVES CONGAR

All those who, in whatever time and place of human history,
respond internally to God's offer of saving grace, are thereby
joined in some degree to the one community of Christian witness;
for their constancy in faith and hope and love is externally manifested in their own times and through the appropriate behavior
patterns of their own people. However obscurely in our eyes, their
lives signify to their neighbors the one true path which leads
redeemed mankind to his destiny. All free human decisions are
significant in relation to God and to man's fulfillment in Him.
But there are degrees of significance. The community of explicit
faith in Christ, which we call the Church of the "latter days,"
contains the fullness of this significance; for she is the primordial
sacrament of mankind's salvation, existing only in order to do
what she signifies, and to signify among all peoples what she is:
the sacramental presence of Christ giving testimony among all
men of what He has already done "once for all" in His historical
presence among some men. This sacramental presence, more or
less manifest, is always among men from the beginning to the
end of creation. "The Church," we read in the Shepherd of

129

Hermas, "was created before all things . . . and for her sake the world was framed." [1] And as St. Augustine has said:

His Body is the Church, not simply the Church that is in this particular place, but both the Church that is here and the Church which extends over the whole earth; not simply the Church that is living today, but the whole race of saints, from Abel down to all those who will ever be born and will believe in Christ.[2]

God's saving love for all men is "always and everywhere"; but His offer of salvation to each man is only in the "here and now" of each one's personal and fleeting experience of earthly existence in the flesh of this or that biological family, in this or that cultural context, in this or that particular place and limited time. Salvation is offered through passing historical events which are tangible and memorable and signal—like those which occurred once on the road leading down from Jerusalem to Jericho, involving a priest, a Levite, and a Samaritan.

The Divine Savior Himself enters into the condition of human bondage in order to re-make all of His creation from within, and to manifest His love to the eyes of flesh and give men hope through faith in the Christ Who is God with us. "He set up his tent among us." In concrete historical terms, He accomplished, in the sight of some men, the salvation of all men. "Once for all at the end of ages, he has appeared for the destruction of sin by the sacrifice of himself . . . offered once to take away the sins of many."[3] His victory is already completed, as he has entered into heaven to appear before God in our behalf. Mankind is already restored to unity in Christ, Who is the Second Adam. This good

---

[1] *The Apostolic Fathers,* tr. and ed. by J. B. Lightfoot, Baker Book House, Grand Rapids, Michigan, 1962, p. 169.

[2] *In Ps.* 90, *sermo* 2, *PL* 37, 1159; quoted by Mersch, *op. cit.,* p. 415.

[3] Heb 9:26–28.

news, however, has not yet reached all men, unambiguously, through historically concrete and relevant symbols.

What remains now to be done in these "latter days" is to make up what is still lacking in comparison with the sufferings already endured, and the victory already achieved, by Christ. Because of the human condition, this also must be done *once for all* in the spatio-temporal dimensions of history, and in the real flesh of men. The first advent of the Messiah was through an historical remnant of God's chosen people in the flesh. The Second Coming is through a sacramental remnant of His chosen people in the spirit: those who are called out of every nation to form the new people of God in the visible community of explicit Christian faith and intelligible witness to their belief before all men. This community is the Church, becoming in the extension of different times and places what she is: the "incarnate" sign of Christ's presence among all peoples, signifying and completing symbolically His universal work of salvation, doing sacramentally among each people what He has done historically once for all.

In union with the historic and trans-historic Christ, this community of explicit faith gives testimony to the universal reality of the messianic Kingdom within all those who have already responded, or shall ever respond, to God's offer of saving grace made available in and through Christ to all mankind. This community is the historical manifestation, through universal symbolism, of the New Israel already existing through hidden grace everywhere in the present order of redeemed mankind. It is the community of Christian witnesses, the visible first fruits of salvation, designated beforehand by God for this very purpose, standing sacramentally for and among the whole people of God. But this community has not yet been completed. All of its previously designated members have not yet been called out from among the nations. And what of those whose explicit faith in Christ is already a tangible foretaste of deliverance and a pledge of hope for all the world? These are the actual "here and now" witnesses, ourselves among them, who are called by God to be the sacramental *Lumen Gentium,* beginning in Jerusalem and extending to the very ends of the earth:

I have an errand for them, to be my messengers across the sea . . . where men never heard of my name . . . And out of all the nations they shall bring your brethren back.[4]

There is something essentially pragmatic in our very notion of witness. One may be summoned as a witness, as we have been by Baptism; but one is actually a witness only when giving his testimony before those who do not yet know the truth of the matter; and one is a true witness only to the extent of his manifesting the whole truth before those who have the right of hearing it. The Christian is called to give his testimony universally, and his duty ceases only with the final witness of his own death. So also, the missionary activity of the Church is something pragmatic. It is a pragmatic test of explicit Christian faith which is given to some men for the sake of actualizing the same latency in other men among whom Christ has not yet been named. This has been said very well by Paul Tillich in describing missions as "that activity of the Church by which it works for the transformation of its own latency into its own manifestation all over the world."[5] He continues:

The action of missions gives the pragmatic proof of the universality of Christianity. It is a *pragmatic* proof. It is the proof, as the Bible calls it, of power and Spirit. It is not a theoretical proof which you can give sitting in your chair, looking at history. . . .

[4] Is 66:19–20.
[5] "Missions and World History," by Paul Tillich, *The Theology of the Christian Mission,* ed. by G. H. Anderson, McGraw-Hill, New York, 1961, p. 283.

The element of faith is always present, and faith is a risk. But a risk must be justified, and that is what missions does. . . . Missions is the continuous pragmatic test of the universality . . . of the truth of the Christian assertion that Jesus is the Christ.[6]

Do we really believe that He is the Messiah for whom the nations are still waiting? Where there is no longer any interest in missionary activity directed to the peoples who have not yet known Christ, there is no Christian faith. There remains only a painted corpse in a crumbling mausoleum. But even this signifies something, if only the presence of a local "tribal religion," and the once-for-allness of Christ's sacramental presence *once* in the past among this particular people. Their situation brings to mind St. Augustine's well known comment that there are many who appear to be outside the Church but are really inside, and there are many who appear to be inside but are really outside.

The universality of Christianity is made manifest only by the universal witness of Christians united visibly, and through historical continuity, with the original apostolic community founded by Christ Himself. This is done by Christians testifying in their conduct to the reunion of all mankind in Christ; and by signifying this symbolically through the activity of making Christ in His visible Church sacramentally present once for all among each of the distinctive ethnic-culture units of people who make up mankind in the here and now of history.

1. The Reunion of Mankind

The whole economy of man's fall and reunion is something foreknown and pre-ordained by God, Who sees and does all in one sweeping vision-act; and this act includes at once everything and

[6] *Ibid.*, p. 286.

every event from the beginning to the end of mankind's corporate, individual, and recapitulated experience of life in the gradually unfolding condition of history. Salvation is offered in the individuated and consecutive terms of this condition; but it is offered to and for mankind as such, because of our ontological involvement in one another. Christianity is, therefore, no mere individual affair providing salvation and consolation for a few chosen souls who, through an "accident of history," happen to live their short lives among that minority of men within the "little flock" of the visible Church. Their call to the life of explicit faith in this sacramental community is not for themselves alone, but for all mankind. Their tangible community actions, as, for example, in the liturgy, are symbolically social actions offered for and by mankind, standing as one new man in Christ before God. This is the burden and the glory of being among the first fruits offered to God by the First Born of all creation, Who was Himself offered for all.

The Christian is more than his "brother's keeper." He is his brother. He does not say of suffering and faithless men: "There but for the grace of God go I." He says: "There go I." He is enriched by every birth and diminished by every death among men. As regards our common destiny in relation to God, and accomplished through Christ, "there is a closer union between our soul and that of our neighbor than between our soul and our body."[7] So Dostoevsky could say through Father Zossima in *The Brothers Karamazov*:

There is only one means of salvation, then take and make yourself responsible for all men's sins . . . for as soon as you sincerely make yourself responsible for everything and for all men, you will see at once that it is really so, and that you are to blame for everyone and

----

[7] *Summa Theol.*, II–II, q. 26, a. 5, ad 2.

for all things. But throwing your own indolence and impotence on others you will end by sharing the pride of Satan and murmuring against God.[8]

And John XXIII could say it also with direct reference to a concrete human situation facing the Christian conscience here and now:

We are all equally responsible for the undernourished peoples. Therefore, it is necessary to educate one's conscience to the sense of responsibility which weighs on each and everyone, especially on those who are more blessed with this world's goods.[9]

All of this is true because the Christian is one who has been chosen by God to stand visibly with Christ for the whole of mankind re-united by Him. Even unto death, He offers Himself for all, that all might share in His one life. And for this has He made Himself responsible for all, the servant of all: the Good Shepherd calling back to visible unity not merely individual sheep who have gone astray, but calling back the whole of mankind still scattered through history among the peoples of the world, gathering together "the elect from the four winds."[10] This is why so many of the early Fathers saw in the story of the Good Shepherd something rather different from what we have been accustomed to see:

For Iranaeus . . . for Origen, Gregory Nazianzen, Gregory of Nyssa, for Cyril of Alexandria, Maximus, Hilary and others the lost sheep of the Gospel that the Good Shepherd brings back to the fold is no other than the whole human nature; its sorry state so moved the

---

[8] *The Brothers Karamazov,* Random House edition, New York, 1950, p. 384.

[9] Quoted by Oliver Barres, *World Mission Windows,* Alba House, New York, 1963, p. 30.

[10] Mk 13:27.

Word of God that He leaves the great flock of angels . . . in order to go to its help.[11]

The "lost sheep" is mankind who by his original sin has been broken into fragments and scattered among the peoples over the face of the earth, and spread out from the beginning to the end of historical time. The Good Shepherd calls them back with the voice of His saving grace, "enlightening every man who comes into the world."[12] His own hear Him, and return in their hearts, through their inner response to grace. But because of what they are in their human condition—corporeal beings of limited space and time, and because of God's incarnational way of saving mankind, they must also return to the fold in the visible tangibility of history. Among each people there is a "remnant" who will actually return in this way before the end. The members of the remnant stand symbolically for all the others of their own people, and of mankind as a whole, who have or shall return in the invisibility of their inner response to saving grace. Like the "remnant" of the old Israel, they stand for and represent the totality of the new people of God. They do this sacramentally among the nations. They are the "remnant" still scattered among the nations, waiting for the "signal" which shall call them home.

So it is in our time; a remnant has remained true; grace has chosen it. . . . Israel has missed the mark; only this chosen remnant has attained it, while the rest were blinded.[13]

While many are called to salvation, only a remnant is chosen to recognize through explicit faith the historical reality of this salvation in Christ, and to give testimony by their hope and love. They signify the vast inner reality of the Kingdom of God

[11] Henri de Lubac in *Catholicism*, p. 3.
[12] Jn 1:9.   [13] Rom 11:5–7.

among men. They are "the messianic people" who, although *they do not actually include all men,* stand as the symbolic representative of all.[14]

An ever diminishing remnant of the Old Israel was sufficient for God's purpose of redeeming all mankind historically through Christ. Is more than this required for the sacramental completion of this work in different times and places? In Oscar Cullmann's concise treatment of this notion of the remnant,[15] we see the progressive reduction of the faithful remnant of Israel, "from the many to the One," Who is the final and central focal point in the historical achievement of mankind's salvation. Then, for the sacramental signification and completion of this work in the extension of different times and places, there is the progressive advance in the "latter days"—"from the One to the many." It is important to note, however—and this is a point on which Cullmann is oddly silent in this same context—that this "many" is not among one particular people, nor among one segment only of mankind. The dynamic orientation of the first Christian community, as indicated in the events of Pentecost and in the Acts of the Apostles, was outward to all peoples—to call home the chosen disciples from every nation. For this reason, Karl Barth's comments on Matthew 28:16–20 are quite relevant. He tells us that "all nations" means "first of all, *people* from among all nations." It is these people, not their nations, who are received into discipleship:

They become *significant* for the existence of their respective nations because the nations now come within the reach of the apostolate and its proclamation and receive their concealed center through the Christian community living in their midst. . . .

---

[14] *Dogmatic Constitution on the Church,* II, 9.
[15] *Christ and Time,* by Oscar Cullman, Westminster, 1950, pp. 115–118.

Not the nations as such are made disciples. This interpretation once infested missionary thinking and was connected with the painful fantasies of the German Christians. It is worthless.[16]

While the actual number of Christian disciples in the world is truly very large and continually increasing, they are nevertheless in quantity a diminishing remnant when considered in relation to the total population of mankind. The important point is that this faithful remnant, this "little flock," is to be *significantly* present as witnesses among the nations. We must desire and work for the numerical increase of the Church everywhere. But we believe that the messianic mission shall have been completed, and the way prepared for the return of the Lord, when a sufficiently significant remnant has made Christ sacramentally present once for all among each people. We are concerned here specifically with the attainable goals of the Church's missionary activity. In this context, therefore, priority in action and organization must be given to the work of establishing the visible Church through "calling out" a nucleus of chosen disciples from among all peoples who have not yet been evangelized once for all. These disciples will be the significant remnant among their own peoples, an ever increasing light calling more and more of their own; but equally and at the same time they will be a light to all nations.

So we see that the Church is "a gathering of men among other gatherings of men," a representative people standing for the whole people of God, and interceding explicitly through Christ for all men. The Church, existing indigenously in this or that particular nation, stands for the whole people, including all who have lived or shall live as members of this particular people; for all of them form together one people through their biological, cultural, and

[16] "An Exegetical Study of Matthew 28:16–20," by Karl Barth, *The Theology of the Christian Mission*, p. 64.

historical continuity; and the whole work of saving-grace is recapitulated sacramentally in the Church among them, even as Christ recapitulated all historically. Thus de Lubac could say in a very significant passage:

When a missionary proclaims Christ to a people that does not yet know him, it is not only those men or their *desendants* that hear his preaching, who are concerned with the success of his mission. It is also, and it can be said in more than one sense, their *ancestors*. Indirectly, but really it is the whole nameless mass of those who, from the beginnings of our race, have done their best in that darkness or half light that was their lot. And so it is that God, desiring that all men should be saved, but not allowing in practice that all should be visibly in the Church, wills nevertheless that all those who answer his call should in the last resort be saved through his Church. . . .[17]

Perhaps this also casts some light on the meaning of St. Peter's mysterious words about the Gospel being preached "even to the dead,"[18] and on the meaning of the Psalmist's words:

The furthest dwellers on earth will bethink themselves of the Lord . . . all the families of the nations will worship before Him. . . . Him shall they worship . . . *that are laid to rest in the earth,* even from their dust, they shall adore Him. I, too, shall live in His presence, and beget children to serve Him . . . and they shall announce His justice to people *yet to be born.*[19]

We must now consider all of this in the concrete terms of our own human psychology.

2. Sacramentally Symbolized

The reunion of mankind in Christ, and the recapitulation of all things in Him, is the reality to which Christians as a community give witness in the living sacramental symbolism of their lives

[17] *Op. cit.,* p. 117. [18] 1 Pt 3:19–20; 4:6.
[19] Ps 21:28–32.

while human history unfolds. The Kingdom of God is within all those who, foreknown and predestined and called and justified,[20] respond to grace from the beginning to the end of mankind's total history; and who thus gradually restore man's likeness to God, in their conformity to the image of His son;[21] for this "likeness to God" is man in his universal community, not in his isolated individuality. And the universal community of men, internally responding to grace, is the true people of God, though not yet visibly so. They will be seen for what they are only at the end, in direct historical visibility, when they also shall be glorified in Christ's glory, when history shall have been fully unfolded.

In the meantime, while awaiting the end of history and the final Parousia, the reality of this Kingdom and inner unity is made visible only symbolically—as a foretaste and pledge—through the presence of the Church (the sacramental Parousia) doing once for all, in the signified visibility of different historical times and places, what Christ has done once for all in actuality. The Church is the faithful remnant of God's people, the new people who are called to bear witness to what God has done through Christ. This faithful remnant among the nations is destined to become the universally tangible Church among the nations, standing symbolically for all the others with whom it is one in the redeeming Christ, and signifying among each people the salvation of all who ever have believed or shall believe through invisible grace. The visible members of the Church, these conscious witnesses to the reality of grace, are the first fruits, in historical terms, of the reality of God's all-embracing will to save mankind. They are the sign to be raised up among the peoples

[20] Rom 8:29–30.   [21] *Ibid.*

who have not yet produced, by explicit faith in Christ, the visible first fruits of their own people's salvation.

The Church among the nations is the sacramental sign of mankind's salvation.[22] A sacramental sign stands *symbolically* for what it signifies. It does what it signifies because it is the very reality signified; it is the reality, but in a different mode of existence; it is the reality, but not yet in its fullness. *Symbolism* is the Church's relevant mode of existence on earth. It is enough of the inner reality, for which it stands, to convey and to signify its meaning.

The symbolic action of two men shaking hands signifies the inner affection of two friends. This outward gesture is more than just a natural manifestation of the inner disposition; it also contributes, in a causal way, to the vitality of the disposition from which it arises and which it signifies—provided only that the disposition of friendship is already present and mutual. One may consider another example in the loving embrace of a mother and her child. This is a natural symbolic action of universally valid significance. The inner realities of existence are, of themselves, neither visible nor measurable; they are only signified to us by fleeting human gestures and passing historical forms which we call symbols. But these symbolic manifestations of meaning are immediate, primordial, self-contained, intrinsic, and universal.

The solidarity of mankind is manifest through the existing communities in which men identify themselves as "the people." These communities are mankind symbolically and really. The tangible presence of the Church within the histories of these peoples is the symbol of mankind's union in Christ, Who is at once the Head of the Church and the Head of mankind. For the

---

[22] *Dogmatic Constitution on the Church,* I, 1; II, 9; VII, 48.

Church is the new people, called out visibly from among these different ethnic-culture units of men and standing symbolically for all men of every nation. This visible people of God is, in sacramental representation, the whole of redeemed mankind; but this sacramental symbol has not yet been completed historically in the sight and in the hearing of all men. Through the Church, visibly present among one people after another, God symbolically embraces all mankind in historically tangible terms—although all are already in His embrace, invisibly. From the viewpoint of the Church's universally valid symbolism, it is enough that the indigenously established community of explicit Christian faith should exist *once for all* among one people after another in the consecutive and individuated and eschatological terms of man's total history in which all of the distinctive peoples scattered over time and place are always the one and same redeemed mankind. This is why all of the Church's sacramental action is essentially social. Each historically separate sacramental enactment is for all men, and signifies and accomplishes historically the manifestation of God's universally salvific will—that same salvific will which is at work always through the inner instincts of men everywhere in the eschatologically oriented condition of redeemed mankind.

How can we express in concrete ways this representative nature of the Church and this once-for-allness of her historical presence and action among men? The Church's historical existence is, as we have seen, rooted in those biological, sociological, and psychological realities which are embraced in the scriptural notion of the "tribes and tongues and peoples and nations." Let us consider the Church's saving significance for a particular people among whom she exists visibly at a certain point in their history. We may do this by making use of Yves Congar's analogy relating to the experience of the French people during the Second World War. By following his comparison between the Church in a nation and the French resistance movement called the *Maquis,* we see how the Church may be truly present to a whole people (including all the past, present, and future members of this people) without consciously embracing every single individual person in the ethnic-culture community.

A king has been forced to seek refuge in a free country; his own kingdom is occupied by invaders. From this far land he prepared a counter-invasion in force that shall achieve complete liberation. Meanwhile, in the occupied country, many people have come to terms with the invaders and even work with them. Most of the people live from day to day, as best they can, waiting for deliverance. . . .

But a certain number of men and women actively reject the enemy's yoke . . . These resisters, amid great hardships, strive to live as subjects of the free motherland they hope for and of their king. They are tireless in their efforts toward liberation; and they are successful in enlisting the help of quite a lot of the half-indifferent, who give support to the resisters from time to time. But the resisters are disinterested men; they work for the liberation and happiness of everyone, without distinction.

When the counter-invasion comes about, deliverance will be due to the resisters *as well as* to the regular military operations. Those people who have had no contacts with them or have despised and opposed them, will see in the resisters the first fruits of their recovered freedom: a group representing themselves, who through every trial have kept alive the possibility of a happy future for *all.* This "all," however, will not mean every single individual, for a number of proved "collaborators" and traitors will be punished, but "all" in the sense of the general whole as such.[23]

These were truly representative events which occurred once for all among the French people, involving not only the people of the present, but also those of the past and of the future. The

[23] *The Wide World, My Parish,* by Yves Congar, O.P., Helicon, Baltimore, 1961, pp. 25–26.

heroic resisters, the faithful remnant, could not have acted as they did were it not for the distinctive heritage which had been gradually formed and handed down to them by their progenitors; nor would they have acted as they did, were they not moved by a common will to pass on this inheritance, now enriched, to the future members of their own people. Their actions had to refer both to the past and to the future, because the *whole* people is saved only for and through the whole people. This totality is symbolical. Some individual men may be lost. Damnation, unlike salvation, is always the unique achievement of the individual in selfish isolation from the community of his historical destiny. So it is with the Church among a people. All the people are one in this symbolical totality, even though only a remnant stands visibly for them, which embraces both past and future in a history of eschatological events.

This story of the *Maquis* is one way of putting it. But, together with all that we have said in the pages of this book, it points to the missionary significance of the peoples who have not yet been evangelized; and it suggests the prior urgency of the whole Church's obligation to become, in proportion to our present resources in the here and now of history, the sacramental *Lumen Gentium*. For this Gospel must *first* be preached for a witness among every people, and *then* shall the end come; and *then* shall the Lord return. Indeed, as Oscar Cullmann has said, "the missionary work of the Church is the eschatological foretaste of the Kingdom of God, and the biblical hope of the 'end' constitutes the keenest incentive to action."[24] And St. Augustine inquired:

Our Spouse is absent; examine your conscience: do you want Him to come, or do you want Him to delay a little longer?[25]

[24] "Eschatology and Missions in the New Testament," by Oscar Cullmann, *The Theology of the Christian Mission,* p. 43.

[25] *Enerratio in Ps.* 127:8–9; *PL* 37, 1681–1682.